GACE

Middle Grades Language Arts Practice Questions

DEAR FUTURE EXAM SUCCESS STORY

First of all, **THANK YOU** for purchasing Mometrix study materials!

Second, congratulations! You are one of the few determined test-takers who are committed to doing whatever it takes to excel on your exam. **You have come to the right place.** We developed these practice tests with one goal in mind: to deliver you the best possible approximation of the questions you will see on test day.

Standardized testing is one of the biggest obstacles on your road to success, which only increases the importance of doing well in the high-pressure, high-stakes environment of test day. Your results on this test could have a significant impact on your future, and these practice tests will give you the repetitions you need to build your familiarity and confidence with the test content and format to help you achieve your full potential on test day.

Your success is our success

We would love to hear from you! If you would like to share the story of your exam success or if you have any questions or comments in regard to our products, please contact us at **800-673-8175** or **support@mometrix.com**.

Thanks again for your business and we wish you continued success!

Sincerely,
The Mometrix Test Preparation Team

TABLE OF CONTENTS

Practice Test #1

1. Which author of young adult fiction won the Newbery Medal for her novel *A Wrinkle in Time*?

    a.   Lois Lowry
    b.   J. K. Rowling
    c.   Ursula K. Le Guin
    d.   Madeleine L'Engle

2. Which of the following authors was a 19th-century British novelist and short-story writer?

    a.   O. Henry
    b.   Charles Dickens
    c.   Herman Melville
    d.   Nathaniel Hawthorne

3. Of the following classic works, which one is NOT an epic poem?

    a.   *Beowulf*
    b.   *The Odyssey*
    c.   *Divine Comedy*
    d.   *The Decameron*

4. What is the correct terminology for a group of related ideas, expressed in multiple lines of text, and separated from other such groups by spaces, in the genre of poetry?

    a.   Verse
    b.   Stanza
    c.   Refrain
    d.   Paragraph

5. Among these literary genres, in which pair has one *most* been used within the other?

    a.   Nonfiction prose within poetry
    b.   Fictional prose within drama
    c.   Poetry within fictional drama
    d.   Poetry within nonfiction prose

6. The term *soliloquy* is used to refer to an element typically found in which literary genre/subgenre?

    a.   Drama
    b.   Poetry
    c.   Novels
    d.   Essays

7. Which pair contains terms typically applied to two subgenres of *two different* literary genres, rather than to two subgenres of the *same single* literary genre?

    a.   Picaresque and epistolary
    b.   Historical and speculative
    c.   Persuasive and expository
    d.   Bildungsroman and elegy

8. Among genres of literature, which is typically the most condensed or verbally economical?

    a. A play
    b. A novel
    c. A poem
    d. An essay

9. Of the following titles, which is/are both written in actual essay form AND of essay length, i.e., shorter than book length? Select ALL correct answers.

    a. An Essay on Man
    b. An Essay on Criticism
    c. An Essay on the Shaking Palsy
    d. An Essay on the Principle of Population
    e. An Essay Concerning Human Understanding

10. Which of these elements is LESS likely to be found in drama and in all genres of literature?

    a. Characters
    b. Narrative
    c. Conflict
    d. Action

11. Among the following, which describes a characteristic that the literary genres of satire and realism both share in common?

    a. Ethical issues are often addressed.
    b. Behaviors are often exaggerated.
    c. Language used is straightforward.
    d. Exposure wins over verisimilitude.

12. In comparing and contrasting the sonnet and the ballad as subgenres of the literary genre of poetry, which of these do both forms have in common?

    a. They both have five main kinds.
    b. They both often express love.
    c. They both began with music.
    d. They both have equal meter.

13. What is a primary distinction between the fiction subgenres of historical fiction and science fiction?

    a. One is set in the real past; the other is set in the possible future.
    b. One is based on facts; the other is based on speculations.
    c. One is concerned with events; the other is concerned with inventions.
    d. Answers (a) and (b) both apply; (c) is not necessarily true.

14. Which two subgenres of nonfiction commonly share content type but not authorship type?

    a. Biography and autobiography
    b. Persuasive and informational
    c. Informational and biography
    d. Autobiography and persuasive

15. Of the following, which technique is NOT commonly shared by both satire and realism?

a. Writing that utilizes a serious tone
b. Exaggerating situations and ideas
c. Portraying irony in situations
d. Writing vernacular dialogue

16. In *Great Expectations,* among relationships involving conflicts that Dickens used to develop the theme of revenge, which choice correctly describes how revenge figured in the relationship?

a. Miss Havisham takes her revenge against Estella.
b. Estella takes her revenge against Miss Havisham.
c. Magwitch takes revenge against protagonist Pip.
d. Pip takes his revenge against the character Orlick.

17. Which of the following use(s) figurative meaning rather than literal meaning?

a. The willow tree has long branches that trail.
b. The willow tree's leaves look like teardrops.
c. The willow tree is weeping into the stream.
d. Options (b) and (c) are figurative, while (a) is literal.

18. In which of the following literary works is the first-person narrative told by the main character?

a. *Sherlock Holmes* by Sir Arthur Conan Doyle
b. *The Tell-Tale Heart* by Edgar Allan Poe
c. *Gulliver's Travels* by Jonathan Swift
d. In (b) and (c), but not in (a)

19. Which of these best represents a main theme in William Shakespeare's *Romeo and Juliet?*

a. Teenage love will always lead to tragedy.
b. Defying society may have fatal results.
c. Love and violence are unrelated entities.
d. Fate does not control those who defy it.

20. In his poem "The Eagle," Alfred Tennyson includes this verse: "He clasps the crag with crooked hands." This incorporates which types of figurative language? Select all choices that apply.

a. Simile
b. Imagery
c. Metaphor
d. Alliteration
e. Personification

21. When students read informational text, they must be able to connect it with their existing knowledge and draw inferences from it to do which of the following?

    a. Comprehend the material enough to make conclusions, critical judgments, and interpretations

    b. Comprehend the material in the informational text thoroughly without doing anything further

    c. Comprehend the material and then make conclusions about it instead of any critical judgment

    d. Comprehend the material and produce their own interpretations of it rather than conclusions

22. In which of the following examples has the author created an instance of situational irony?

    a. In *Great Expectations,* Pip and the readers think Miss Havisham is his benefactor, but it is Magwitch.

    b. In *The Cask of Amontillado,* Fortunato says a cough won't kill him; Montresor replies, "True—true."

    c. In *Romeo and Juliet,* Romeo, without the Friar's letter, thinks Juliet is dead; readers know she is alive.

    d. In every one of these examples, the irony created is dramatic rather than verbal or situational irony.

23. In *The Old Man and the Sea,* Hemingway begins, "He was an old man who fished alone in a skiff in the Gulf Stream and he had gone eighty-four days now without taking a fish." The primary meaning of this opening sentence is

    a. symbolic

    b. implied

    c. literal

    d. true

24. From this passage, which of the following can the reader most accurately infer?

> Mamzelle Aurélie had never thought of marrying. She had never been in love. At the age of 20, she had received a proposal, which she had promptly declined, and at the age of 50 she had not yet lived to regret it.
> (from "Regret" by Kate Chopin)

    a. Mamzelle Aurélie was certainly lonesome.

    b. Mamzelle Aurélie was quite independent.

    c. Mamzelle Aurélie was changing her mind.

    d. Mamzelle Aurélie was sorry to be unwed.

Answer the next three questions based on the following passage:

When students miss class, not only do they lose out on important instructional time, but they also miss opportunities to build critical connections with other students and adults. While students are identified as truant when they miss multiple unexcused days of school in a row, students who miss many nonsequential days (excused or unexcused) can fly under the radar. When these absences add up to more or a month or more of school, students are considered "chronically absent." At a national level, an estimated 7.5 million students are considered chronically absent each year. In some states, this translates to 1 in 5 students that do not regularly attend.

While missing one or two days of school each month may seem like a nonissue, time away can quickly accumulate and negatively impact mathematics and reading achievement during that school year as well as in the years that follow. For example, chronic absence in kindergarten has a negative impact on academic performance and socioemotional skills, critical building blocks to success.

— Lauren Mims, Fellow, White House Initiative on Educational Excellence,
HOMEROOM – official US Department of Education blog, 10/07/2015

25. According to the textual evidence, what differentiates chronic absence from truancy?
   a. The number of school days a student is absent
   b. Whether the absences are excused/unexcused
   c. Sequential versus nonsequential student absence
   d. The excerpt has no textual evidence about this.

26. Where in this passage is there textual evidence supporting the position that chronic absence is a serious issue by citing statistics?
   a. The passage has none.
   b. In the first paragraph
   c. In the second paragraph
   d. In the third paragraph

27. What textual evidence does the author provide to support her statement that missing one or two days of school each month is not the nonissue it seems to be?
   a. Statistics showing the national volume of chronic absences
   b. A generalized example of the negative impacts of absences
   c. None; she simply states it without any supporting evidence.
   d. A differential definition of chronic absences versus truancy

28. In his short story "The Tell-Tale Heart," Edgar Allan Poe has the main character narrate the tale in the first person. What impact does this have relative to the character's and readers' point of view?
   a. It helps readers to identify with the main character.
   b. It enables readers to sympathize with the narrator.
   c. It lends narrator credibility via a firsthand account.
   d. It emphasizes the character's divorce from reality.

Answer the next two questions based on the following quotation:

Edward Bulwer-Lytton's 1830 novel *Paul Clifford* opens, "It was a dark and stormy night; the rain fell in torrents—except at occasional intervals, when it was checked by a violent gust of wind which swept up the streets...rattling along the housetops, and fiercely agitating the scanty flame of the lamps that struggled against the darkness."

29. The author's establishment of the setting contributes most to which of the following literary elements?
   a. Plot
   b. Tone
   c. Mood
   d. Conflict

5

30. In the author's word choices that make this sentence more descriptive, the majority of the arguably most descriptive words are which part of speech?

    a. Verbs
    b. Nouns
    c. Adverbs
    d. Adjectives

Answer the next three questions based on the following poem:

O Ship of State

by Henry Wadsworth Longfellow

Thou, too, sail on, O Ship of State!

Sail on, O Union, strong and great!

Humanity with all its fears,

With all the hopes of future years,

Is hanging breathless on thy fate!

We know what Master laid thy keel,

What Workmen wrought thy ribs of steel,

Who made each mast, and sail, and rope,

What anvils rang, what hammers beat,

In what a forge and what a heat

Were shaped the anchors of thy hope!

Fear not each sudden sound and shock,

'Tis of the wave and not the rock;

'Tis but the flapping of the sail,

And not a rent made by the gale!

In spite of rock and tempest's roar,

In spite of false lights on the shore,

Sail on, nor fear to breast the sea!

Our hearts, our hopes, are all with thee.

Our hearts, our hopes, our prayers, our tears,

Our faith triumphant o'er our fears,

Are all with thee,—are all with thee!

31. This poem overall is an example of the use of which literary figurative language?

    a. A single metaphor
    b. Extended metaphor
    c. The use of a simile
    d. Use of vivid imagery

32. What is the meter of this poem?

    a. Iambic pentameter
    b. Anapestic tetrameter
    c. Iambic tetrameter
    d. Dactylic dimeter

33. How do the rhyme and meter of this poem contribute to its meaning?

    a. Their regularity reinforces the idea of steady strength.
    b. Their unevenness emphasizes the theme of insecurity.
    c. Their monotony establishes a sense of the unchanging.
    d. Their choppiness mirrors the images of the stormy sea.

34. In the two-column notes active reading strategy, using Lincoln's Gettysburg Address as an example, which of the following clauses or phrases would go under the column of main ideas?

    a. "Four score and seven years ago"
    b. "Our fathers brought forth... a new nation"
    c. "Conceived in Liberty"
    d. "Dedicated to the proposition that all men are created equal."

35. Among the following techniques whereby authors of informational text connect and distinguish ideas, which one is capable of showing both similarities *and* differences?

    a. Comparing
    b. Analogizing
    c. Contrasting
    d. Categorizing

36. Which of the following statements is/are true about a glossary and an index in an informational text? Select all choices that apply.

    a. Only one is in alphabetical order.
    b. Only one is in the back of a book.
    c. Only one lists a book's main topics.
    d. Only one lists entries' page numbers.
    e. Only one provides definitions of terms.

37. Which of the following sentences uses the underlined word for a connotative rather than denotative meaning?

    a. Asked where his homework was, he gave a smart retort.
    b. Sandy got detention for having a smart mouth all period.
    c. Wendell was smart to arrive early on the day of the test.
    d. (a) and (b) use the connotation, but (c) uses denotation.

38. How should technical language used in a scientific informational text differ from vernacular (everyday) or literary language used in other texts? Select all choices that apply.

    a. It should be more grandiose.
    b. It should be more impersonal.
    c. It should be more professional.
    d. It should be more self-deprecating.
    e. It should always be in passive voice.

39. Which of the following is true about the author's point of view or purpose in an informational text?

    a. Readers can always identify this because informational authors state it explicitly.
    b. Readers will have to infer this when an informational author never identifies it.
    c. Readers can identify it equally from neutral, balanced, or opinionated positions.
    d. Readers who have to analyze text to identify this can assume it is poorly written.

40. If an author of informational text makes a reference to someone famous, e.g., the name of a literary or historical figure, to create resonance with readers and/or make something or someone in the text symbolic, what rhetorical device is this?

    a. Allusion
    b. Paradox
    c. Analogy
    d. Parody

41. Shakespeare wrote in Act II, Scene VII of *As You Like It*: "All the world's a stage, /And all the men and women merely players;/They have their exits and their entrances;/And one man in his time plays many parts ...." His meaning here is _____.

    a. primarily denotative
    b. primarily connotative
    c. half one, half the other
    d. neither type of meaning

42. Among persuasive methods of appeal, which of the following writing techniques supports the author's views by quoting others who agree with them?

    a. Anticipating objections
    b. Citing expert opinions
    c. Bandwagon appeals
    d. Testimonials

43. Reasons that authors of technical informational text may need to write in non-technical language include which of the following?
- a. To communicate denser content rather than messages
- b. To inform one's colleagues who work in the same field
- c. To procure economic support for budgets and projects
- d. To inform a narrow range of citizens having knowledge

44. What most accurately represents some of the steps to take and their sequence for readers to evaluate arguments in informational text?
- a. Readers should identify premises supporting an argument's conclusion first, and then the conclusion.
- b. Readers should identify an argument's conclusion first, and then identify the premises supporting it.
- c. Readers should list an argument's conclusion and supporting premises in their order of identification.
- d. Readers should try to paraphrase premises to clarify them, not to make them fit with the conclusion.

45. Which statement is most accurate about reader identification of author purpose in informational writing?
- a. Considering why an author wrote a text affords greater insights into it
- b. Considering why an author wrote a text inhibits critical reading skills
- c. Considering why an author wrote a text inhibits reader expectations
- d. Considering why an author wrote a text allows less reader response

46. Among the following, what defines an adverb as a part of speech?
- a. It serves to name a person, place, or thing
- b. It serves to name an action or state of being
- c. It modifies a verb, adjective, or another adverb
- d. It modifies or describes a noun or adjective

47. Which of these most accurately represents persuasive techniques used in various media for advertising?
- a. Persuasion via humor is used more often in news and advocacy than in advertising.
- b. Qualifiers, better known as "weasel words," typically accompany understatement.
- c. Hyperbole (exaggeration), superlatives, and other intensifiers are least persuasive.
- d. Repetition and appeals to audience sentiment are both effective persuasive tools.

48. In an informational text, which of these is most likely to make use of the others?
- a. Irony
- b. Satire
- c. Overstatement
- d. Understatement

49. A word that can modify a verb, an adjective, or an adverb is _____ .
- a. An adjective
- b. An adverb
- c. A noun
- d. A verb

50. The sentence, "After completing the assignment correctly, the teacher gave Peter a high grade" is an example of which kind of error?

    a. A lack of parallelism
    b. A sentence fragment
    c. A dangling participle
    d. A run-on sentence

51. Which version of this sentence is most correctly punctuated and worded?

    a. "Discussing the plan, Maddie and David disagreed, they often had differences of opinion."
    b. "Discussing the plan, Maddie and David disagreed; they often had differences of opinion."
    c. "Discussing the plan, Maddie and David disagreed. They often had differences of opinion."
    d. "Discussing the plan, Maddie and David disagreed; and they often had differences of opinion."

52. "I would like to go with you; however, I won't have time." In this sentence, what part of speech is the word "however?"

    a. Preposition
    b. Conjunction
    c. Conjunctive adverb
    d. Subordinating conjunction

53. "Although Ted had an impressive education, he had little experience working with individuals, which made him less effective at relating to them." Which kinds of clauses does this sentence contain?

    a. Two dependent clauses and one independent clause
    b. One dependent clause and two independent clauses
    c. Two independent clauses and no dependent clauses
    d. One dependent clause and one independent clause

54. "Every time they visited, she got to know him a little bit better." Which structure does this sentence have?

    a. Simple
    b. Complex
    c. Compound
    d. Compound-complex

55. "The tall man wearing a black raincoat, a yellow hat, and one red shoe entered the restaurant, walked to the back, and sat down alone at the smallest table farthest away from the staff and other patrons." This sentence has which of the following structures?

    a. Simple
    b. Complex
    c. Compound
    d. Compound-complex

56. Teachers must consider student developmental levels when assigning cooperative learning projects and/or discussions. For example, students are bored by topics at younger age levels and lost by topics at older ones. In addition to chronological age, which other developmental level does this example relate to most?

    a. Social developmental levels
    b. Cognitive developmental levels
    c. Emotional developmental levels
    d. Behavioral developmental levels

57. Which of the following suffixes is NOT commonly used to form a noun from some other part of speech?

    a. -ation
    b. -ness
    c. -ity
    d. -id

58. Which of the following reference sources would help a reader find out the meaning of a specialized vocabulary or terminology word in a technical or subject-specific text?

    a. Glossary
    b. Dictionary
    c. Style manual
    d. Spell checker

59. "This behavior signifies not only a decline in manners, but also common sense." What is a grammatical error in this sentence?

    a. A misplaced modifier
    b. A squinting modifier
    c. A dangling participle
    d. There are no errors.

60. "He woke up, looked at the clock, got dressed, ate a hurried breakfast, got into his car, drove downtown, parked the car, walked across the street and up the block to the corner building next to the grocery store, opened the front door, and went inside." What type of sentence is this?

    a. Compound–complex
    b. Compound sentence
    c. A complex sentence
    d. A simple sentence

61. Which of the following is an example of a complex sentence?

    a. I do not have the time, although I would like to go with you.
    b. I would like to go with you; however, I do not have the time.
    c. I would like to be able to make the time to go out with you.
    d. I'd go, and I'd go with you, if only I could just make the time.

62. **"They had planned to be on time; unfortunately, though, unexpected events delayed their arrival." What type of sentence is this?**

    a. A simple sentence
    b. Compound sentence
    c. A complex sentence
    d. Compound–complex

63. **"After David met Marcia, he knew she was the one, and he soon proposed marriage to her." This is what type of sentence?**

    a. It is a compound sentence.
    b. It is a compound–complex sentence.
    c. It is a complex sentence.
    d. It is a simple sentence.

64. **"He went to the _____ in order to _____ what happened." By applying knowledge of syntax, which of these could the reader determine?**

    a. The parts of speech of the missing words
    b. The specific words for filling in the blanks
    c. The reader can determine neither of these.
    d. The reader could determine both of these.

65. **A middle school student notices the vocabulary words *retroactive, retrograde, retrospect, retrospective, retrovirus, retro-rockets,* and *"retro" fashions* in reading school and everyday materials. By knowing the meaning of at least one of these words, the student can determine that the prefix *retro-* means which of the following?**

    a. Backward
    b. Forward
    c. Sideways
    d. Upward

66. **In a rough draft of an essay, a student has written, "My best friend Gina is a wonderful athlete, a wonderful student, a wonderful person, and a wonderful friend." Which online reference should she consult to improve this description?**

    a. A grammar guide
    b. An encyclopedia
    c. A dictionary
    d. A thesaurus

67. **In which mode of writing are authors most likely intent on convincing readers to agree with their belief(s) about a given issue?**

    a. Narrative
    b. Informative
    c. Explanatory
    d. Argumentative

68. Which of the following is a primary function of argumentative writing?

a. To introduce readers to some new information
b. To explain how a process functions to readers
c. To develop an idea or concept for the readers
d. To prove a point that will convince the readers

69. Which statement is most accurate regarding journals as a form of writing?

a. Journals are only for confiding and processing personal experiences in private.
b. Journals need never be edited for mechanics because nobody will ever see them.
c. Journals may be expected or hoped by some authors to be published one day.
d. Journals may be shared with readers, but are never therapeutic for an author.

70. The introduction of an essay should answer three questions. Which of those answers represents the writer's thesis statement?

a. What the subject of the essay will be
b. How the essay addresses the subject
c. How the author structured this essay
d. What this essay is supposed to prove

71. When writing an essay, which is the best way to address multiple main points?

a. Cover all main points, supporting evidence, and its relation to thesis in a single long paragraph.
b. Introduce each point in one paragraph, support it in another, and relate it to the thesis in another.
c. Cover each point, the evidence supporting it, and its relation to the thesis in a separate paragraph.
d. How the writer addresses multiple main points in an essay is completely individual preference.

72. To help students select the content and format they will use in writing, what should teachers include in their instruction?

a. They should have students consider swaying reader opinions more than giving proof.
b. They should have students consider what readers will agree with instead of disagree with.
c. They should have students consider not what to impart, but what their readers know.
d. They should have students consider what information their readers share with them.

73. Regarding organization, what statement is most accurate about outlines relative to writing?

a. Outlining is only for student writers.
b. Outlines are for professional writers.
c. Outlines are for planning, not analyzing.
d. Outlines aid in planning and analysis.

74. Of the following writing practices, which will interfere with producing a good paragraph?

a. Confine the content of each paragraph to only one main idea
b. Develop the main idea in a paragraph by giving specific details
c. Include a great many supporting details: the more, the better
d. Use a specific structural pattern to develop each paragraph

75. Which of the following writing techniques that contribute to paragraph coherence is most related to using matching grammatical constructions within, between, and among sentences?

    a. Repetition
    b. Parallelism
    c. Transitions
    d. Consistency

76. Regarding essay writing, which of these is accurate about the organization of essays?

    a. Well-organized essays are more likely to gain readers' acceptance of their theses as valid.
    b. Well-organized essays have better structure but are less likely to hold readers' attention.
    c. Well-organized essays are easier for writers to compose yet harder for readers to follow.
    d. Well-organized essays give readers better guides, but are harder for writers to compose.

77. Which of these is/are most applicable to differences of online blogs vs. print articles?

    a. Blogs are not expected by readers to be as high in quality as print.
    b. Blogs must be more legible and use more predictive text features.
    c. Blogs afford less complexity to format and write than newspapers.
    d. Blogs can be skimmed by readers the same way as printed articles.

78. Which mode of writing is most suitable for the purpose of encouraging the reading audience to explore ideas and consider various potential associated responses?

    a. Narrative
    b. Expository
    c. Persuasive
    d. Speculative

79. Among the following, which is the best example of writing for certain purposes?

    a. An older student writes in simpler vocabulary, syntax, and printing for younger readers.
    b. A writer's word choice and diction stimulate readers' feelings of empathy and sympathy.
    c. A writer's word choice and diction stimulate readers to challenge opposing viewpoints.
    d. Writers select different (expository, persuasive, narrative, etc.) formats and language.

80. When citing research sources, which of the following must be cited whether the sources are printed or electronic?

    a. Publisher name and publication city
    b. Periodical name, volume, issue, page numbers
    c. Answers (a) and (b) for both print and electronic sources
    d. Database name, database publisher name, URL

68. Which of the following is a primary function of argumentative writing?
   a. To introduce readers to some new information
   b. To explain how a process functions to readers
   c. To develop an idea or concept for the readers
   d. To prove a point that will convince the readers

69. Which statement is most accurate regarding journals as a form of writing?
   a. Journals are only for confiding and processing personal experiences in private.
   b. Journals need never be edited for mechanics because nobody will ever see them.
   c. Journals may be expected or hoped by some authors to be published one day.
   d. Journals may be shared with readers, but are never therapeutic for an author.

70. The introduction of an essay should answer three questions. Which of those answers represents the writer's thesis statement?
   a. What the subject of the essay will be
   b. How the essay addresses the subject
   c. How the author structured this essay
   d. What this essay is supposed to prove

71. When writing an essay, which is the best way to address multiple main points?
   a. Cover all main points, supporting evidence, and its relation to thesis in a single long paragraph.
   b. Introduce each point in one paragraph, support it in another, and relate it to the thesis in another.
   c. Cover each point, the evidence supporting it, and its relation to the thesis in a separate paragraph.
   d. How the writer addresses multiple main points in an essay is completely individual preference.

72. To help students select the content and format they will use in writing, what should teachers include in their instruction?
   a. They should have students consider swaying reader opinions more than giving proof.
   b. They should have students consider what readers will agree with instead of disagree with.
   c. They should have students consider not what to impart, but what their readers know.
   d. They should have students consider what information their readers share with them.

73. Regarding organization, what statement is most accurate about outlines relative to writing?
   a. Outlining is only for student writers.
   b. Outlines are for professional writers.
   c. Outlines are for planning, not analyzing.
   d. Outlines aid in planning and analysis.

74. Of the following writing practices, which will interfere with producing a good paragraph?
   a. Confine the content of each paragraph to only one main idea
   b. Develop the main idea in a paragraph by giving specific details
   c. Include a great many supporting details: the more, the better
   d. Use a specific structural pattern to develop each paragraph

13

75. Which of the following writing techniques that contribute to paragraph coherence is most related to using matching grammatical constructions within, between, and among sentences?

    a. Repetition
    b. Parallelism
    c. Transitions
    d. Consistency

76. Regarding essay writing, which of these is accurate about the organization of essays?

    a. Well-organized essays are more likely to gain readers' acceptance of their theses as valid.
    b. Well-organized essays have better structure but are less likely to hold readers' attention.
    c. Well-organized essays are easier for writers to compose yet harder for readers to follow.
    d. Well-organized essays give readers better guides, but are harder for writers to compose.

77. Which of these is/are most applicable to differences of online blogs vs. print articles?

    a. Blogs are not expected by readers to be as high in quality as print.
    b. Blogs must be more legible and use more predictive text features.
    c. Blogs afford less complexity to format and write than newspapers.
    d. Blogs can be skimmed by readers the same way as printed articles.

78. Which mode of writing is most suitable for the purpose of encouraging the reading audience to explore ideas and consider various potential associated responses?

    a. Narrative
    b. Expository
    c. Persuasive
    d. Speculative

79. Among the following, which is the best example of writing for certain purposes?

    a. An older student writes in simpler vocabulary, syntax, and printing for younger readers.
    b. A writer's word choice and diction stimulate readers' feelings of empathy and sympathy.
    c. A writer's word choice and diction stimulate readers to challenge opposing viewpoints.
    d. Writers select different (expository, persuasive, narrative, etc.) formats and language.

80. When citing research sources, which of the following must be cited whether the sources are printed or electronic?

    a. Publisher name and publication city
    b. Periodical name, volume, issue, page numbers
    c. Answers (a) and (b) for both print and electronic sources
    d. Database name, database publisher name, URL

81. Of the following statements, which one accurately reflects a principle related to integrating source material into research writing?

a. Parenthetically naming studies that agree/disagree with one's position interrupts an argument.
b. If students cannot write an equal/larger number of words about a quotation, it is likely padding.
c. When quoting sources, students should follow quotations with summaries of what these mean.
d. Summarizing others' content is as engaging and original as analyses, syntheses, and evaluations.

82. For effectively giving speeches, which attributes are favorable? Choose ALL correct answers.

a. Formality
b. Directness
c. Confidence
d. Naturalness
e. Theatricality

83. Which of these accurately reflects influences on media choices for giving presentations?

a. Combining more than one type of media is advisable.
b. Experts find it more effective to limit presentations to one medium.
c. Presenters should not let their budgets be influences.
d. The length of communication will not affect the media.

84. What is an accurate reflection of criteria for clear, concise speech presentations?

a. A speaker should not take three or more minutes more to get to the point.
b. A speaker should not pause before answering audience questions.
c. A speaker should include as many anecdotes and details as possible.
d. A speaker should include both necessary and interesting information.

85. Commercials for a mobile service provider frequently reiterate the question, "Can you hear me now?" Which technique of persuasion does this BEST represent?

a. Repetition
b. Slogan use
c. Bandwagon
d. Testimonial

86. MATCHING: Place the correct number from the right-hand column in the corresponding space next to the choice in the left-hand column.

a. Meow Mix® ad uses the song "Meow, meow, meow, meow." ___ 1. Product comparison
b. The words used lack specific meaning, but they sound good. ___ 2. Appealing to reason
c. A brand/product is displayed featuring an American flag. ___ 3. Appealing to emotion
d. A checklist contrasts two brands with/without features. ___ 4. Transfer/association
e. People are seen enjoying quality time involving a brand. ___ 5. Glittering generalities
f. Advertising cites statistics in support of product efficacy. ___ 6. Appeal via repetition

15

87. Common standards for middle school grades include evaluating textual arguments and claims. Within this standard, which of the following is an element applying uniquely to the eighth grade?

    a. Tracing/delineating and evaluating argument and specific claims in a text
    b. Distinguishing claims supported by evidence and reasons versus being unsupported
    c. Assessing whether reasoning is sound and evidence is relevant and sufficient
    d. Recognizing whether some evidence that has been introduced is irrelevant

88. MATCHING: In assessing the soundness of author reasoning, one type of error to look for is a logical fallacy. In the space next to the statement for each letter choice, place the number of the logical fallacy that statement represents.

    a. "Most rapists read pornography as teens; pornography causes rape." 1. Straw man
    b. Of one for strict immigration policy: "He is for killing immigrants." 2. Ad hominem
    c. "Of course she's for affirmative action; she's a minority." 3. Non sequitur
    d. "We need affirmative action because racism is wrong." 4. Post hoc ergo propter hoc

89. Suppose you want to know whether a used car you are looking at is a good vehicle to buy, and the salesperson calls attention to its beautiful paint job. In assessing the relevance of this argument, which of the following applies most?

    a. The paint job is more relevant than the condition of the transmission.
    b. The paint job is less relevant than the fact that the car's frame is bent.
    c. The paint job is more relevant than how well the vehicle's engine runs.
    d. The paint job is less relevant than anything because this is not relevant at all.

90. What is an example of how students can write most appropriately for different tasks, purposes, and audiences?

    a. Using sophisticated language writing for their classmates
    b. Using simple language to request privileges from their parents
    c. Using vivid, entertaining language with younger students
    d. Using humor to ask parent permission for independent activity

91. Suppose a student writes, "My dog is not very bright" as a main point in a composition. Which of the following is an example of additional information that supports this point?

    a. "Every time I leave the house to go to school, he cries."
    b. "When I come home every day, he is always happy to see me."
    c. "At the age of 5 years, he still does not answer to his name."
    d. "He loves to play fetch and will not tire of the game for hours."

92. To provide accommodations for ELL students, which of these should teachers do in vocabulary and reading instruction?

    a. Teach ELL students vocabulary in isolation.
    b. Teach ELL students vocabulary in context.
    c. Teach ELL students vocabulary in volume.
    d. Teach ELL students reading by their speech levels.

93. Of the following statements, which one is accurate regarding teacher promotion and management of active listening and participation by students in collaborative discussions?

    a. For students inexperienced in group discussions, teachers should use topics below their age levels.

    b. To challenge students, teachers should assign group discussion topics above their age levels.

    c. If teachers explain appropriate discussion behaviors first, modeling them becomes unnecessary.

    d. Teachers should model and explain active listening behaviors for students before discussions.

94. Among the following structural patterns in a paragraph, which does a writer use to show readers something instead of telling them something?

    a. Division

    b. Narration

    c. Definition

    d. Description

95. Which of the following is most characteristic of paragraph coherence in writing?

    a. The parts of the paragraph are clearly and discretely separated.

    b. The parts of the paragraph flow well from one part to the next.

    c. Conceptual content is given using contrasting structural patterns.

    d. Control at the sentence level undermines paragraph coherence.

96. Which of the following literary elements are most likely to be found in *both* fictional narratives *and* nonfictional informational text?

    a. The writing style of the author

    b. Labeled diagrams and photos

    c. Excitement and drama

    d. Themes and plots

97. A cohesive written paragraph is described by all EXCEPT which of these characteristics?

    a. Its sentences are unified by ideas that fit together.

    b. Its sentences flow easily from one to the next.

    c. Its sentences connect from old to new information.

    d. Its sentences start with old material and end with new material.

98. Which of these is a fact regarding cohesion and coherence in paragraph writing?

    a. A paragraph can be cohesive but not coherent, not the reverse.

    b. A paragraph can be coherent but not cohesive, not the reverse.

    c. A paragraph can be cohesive but not coherent, or it can be the reverse.

    d. A paragraph that is cohesive is always coherent and also the reverse.

99. To compose cohesive and coherent paragraphs, which of the following should writers do?

    a. Begin sentences by introducing new information

    b. Introduce sentences with long, complex clauses

    c. Make the transitions between ideas transparent

    d. Vary and alternate topics addressed throughout

100. In composing an essay or similar piece, in which sequence should a writer do the following?

a. List all details supporting each main point, organize details in sequential order, narrow topics to a main idea, find which main points support the main idea, decide how to sequence main points

b. Decide how to sequence main points, narrow topics to a main idea, find which main points support the main idea, organize details in sequential order, list all details supporting each main point

c. Organize details in sequential order, decide how to sequence main points, list all details supporting each main point, narrow topics to a main idea, find which main points support the main idea

d. Narrow topics to a main idea, find which main points support the main idea, decide how to sequence main points, list all details supporting each main point, organize details in sequential order

101. Which of the following purposes is/are most applicable to instructional reading strategies and activities conducted *before* students read? Select ALL correct answers.

a. Constructing graphic organizers

b. Activating previous knowledge

c. Determining reading purposes

d. Writing about and discussing the text

e. Discussing vocabulary in the text

102. Based on research evidence, what do experts advocate for effectively instructing students in writing strategies?

a. Teachers should demonstrate strategies and then assign independent student practice.

b. Teachers should explain strategies and let students practice them without any models.

c. Teachers should model strategies, then guide practice, then give independent practice.

d. Teachers should first give students guided practice in strategies and then model them.

103. What do research studies find about student collaboration relative to effective writing instruction?

a. Cooperative learning does not apply to teaching writing.

b. Cooperative learning is an effective practice for writing.

c. Cooperative learning needs no structure from teachers.

d. Cooperative learning needs structure, not expectations.

104. In writing instruction, what does the process writing approach entail?

a. Hypothetical audiences for written work

b. Students work on their own throughout.

c. Personal responsibility for written work

d. Writing is evaluated only by the teacher.

105. Which of the following reflects typical characteristics of formative assessments?

a. They typically use informal methods.

b. They typically have statistical proof.

c. They typically are norm referenced.

d. They typically come after instruction.

106. Relative to formative and summative assessments, research reveals that the single greatest change in classroom instruction for improving student learning and achievement is effective _____, which students and teachers get best from _____ assessments.

 a. comparison; summative
 b. feedback; formative
 c. feedback; summative
 d. comparison; formative

107. Among the following types of tests, which are examples of summative assessments?

 a. Final project critiques
 b. Oral question-and-answer sessions
 c. Running records
 d. Pop quizzes

108. For which of the following purposes would a teacher use a formative assessment?

 a. To get data to inform a school improvement plan
 b. To get or keep government funding for the school
 c. To get data about individual student performance
 d. To get data on student progress over a school year

109. Regarding the strength and closure that a written composition's conclusion should have, which of these indicates a conclusion that does NOT achieve closure?

 a. Readers perceive from the conclusion that the main points made were meaningful and important.
 b. Readers perceive from the conclusion that the writer said what was needed, so the work is complete.
 c. Readers perceive from the conclusion that the writer reached the required word count and stopped.
 d. Readers perceive from the conclusion that evidence supporting main points was well-developed.

110. Which of the following methods would give students the most *objective* feedback to enable them to monitor their own performance and progress in speaking and enacting through giving oral reports and presentations?

 a. Having classmates offer peer reviews
 b. Having a teacher evaluate their work
 c. Comparing their work to classmates' work
 d. Viewing videos of their performance

Constructed Response

1. Textual Interpretation: Based on the following excerpt, write a response answering the questions below it.

> I suppose that the high-water mark of my youth in Columbus, Ohio, was the night the bed fell on my father. It makes a better recitation (unless, as some friends of mine have said, one has heard it five or six times) than it does a piece of writing, for it is almost necessary to throw furniture around, shake doors, and bark like a dog, to lend the proper atmosphere and verisimilitude to what is admittedly a somewhat incredible tale. Still, it did take place.

> (From "The Night the Bed Fell" by James Thurber)

What is the author's narrative point of view?

What is the tone of this opening paragraph? How does Thurber establish it? Give examples.

How does the author use foreshadowing? Give examples.

2. Teaching Writing: Read the following example of a seventh-grade student's essay for a descriptive writing assignment with classmates as the target audience. Based on the essay, write a response addressing the three numbered items below it.

> I find plenty of people important in my life. For example, my parents, my big sister and little brother, the kids in my class and my soccer team, and others. One really important person is my best friend Joe.

> I really care about Joe. Joe is always there for me when I need him. When I'm angry about something, he always gets me to smile. When I'm feeling down, he also gets me to smile. I also like Joe because he is interested in the same things I am. For example, playing sports, music videos, and fantasy football.

> Joe sets a good example. He always tells the truth. He has a lot of good qualities. For example, he is cool, he is funny, he is creative, and I can always count on him. I admire him for being independent and not always doing the same things that everybody else does just to fit in.

> My best friend Joe is important to me for a lot of reasons. When I am with him, he makes me feel like I am more important to him than anybody else. He is a true friend.

1. Identify one strength in the student's writing and give examples from the text that illustrate this strength. Do NOT include grammar, punctuation, or other writing conventions.

2. Identify one weakness in the student's writing and give examples from the text that illustrate this weakness. Do NOT include grammar, punctuation, or other writing conventions.

3. Give a description of one follow-up assignment you could give the student who wrote this essay that would either expand upon the strength you identified in #1 OR remediate the weakness you identified in #2. Explain how this assignment would help the student improve his or her writing.

Answer Key and Explanations

1. D: Madeleine L'Engle (1918–2007) won the Newbery Medal for *A Wrinkle in Time* (1963). Lois Lowry (a) (born 1937) won two Newbery Medals for the historical novel *Number the Stars* (1989) and the young-adult dystopian novel *The Giver* (1993). J.K. Rowling (b) (born 1965), best known for her *Harry Potter* series, has won numerous awards, but not the Newbery Medal (she is British; the others are American). Ursula K. Le Guin (c) (born 1929), best known for her *Earthsea* trilogy, has won a great many awards, including a National Book Award for Young People's Literature, but not the Newbery Medal.

2. B: O. Henry wrote a novel, *Cabbages and Kings,* as well as many short stories. Herman Melville (c) and Nathaniel Hawthorne wrote both novels and short stories. All three were 19th-century American authors. However, Charles Dickens (b), who also wrote novels and short stories, was a 19th-century British author.

3. D: *Beowulf* is an epic poem by an anonymous poet written in Old English (c. 700-1000). The Odyssey (b) is an epic poem orally composed by Homer in ancient Greek (c. 760-700 BC). The Divine Comedy (c) is an epic poem written by Dante Alighieri in Tuscan Italian (1320). *The Decameron* (d) is a series of novellas within a frame tale (like Geoffrey Chaucer's *Canterbury Tales,* which it influenced) rather than an epic poem, written by Giovanni Boccaccio in Florentine Italian (1353).

4. B: The division described in the question is termed a stanza in poetry. A verse (a) is the term for a single line rather than a group of lines in poetry. (In ballads and songs it can mean a group of lines as a stanza does in poems.) A refrain (c) is a line(s), verse(s), or other set of the same or similar words that is/are repeated regularly throughout a ballad, other poem, or song, often alternating with verses. A paragraph (d) is the term for the analogous division, in *prose* only.

5. C: William Shakespeare's plays are good literary examples of poetry within fictional drama because they are written in verse form. Poems typically do not contain inserted prose (a). Plays are not generally known to incorporate pieces of fictional prose (b). Nonfictional prose sometimes incorporates quotations of poetry or even occasionally original poems, but this occurs much less often than with Shakespeare's plays and many others written entirely or mostly in poetry (d).

6. A: A soliloquy is a speech made by one character in a play speaking alone, as opposed to dialogue between/among multiple characters. Some poets (e.g., Robert Browning) have written entire poems in the voice of a single character; however, these are called dramatic monologues rather than soliloquies, a term generally reserved for drama, not poetry (b). Similarly, in novels (c), conversation between/among characters is called dialogue, whereas a long speech by one character would be called a monologue. Essays (d) are typically nonfiction and do not contain characters or their speech.

7. D: A bildungsroman is a term for a novel in which the main character comes of age, develops, learns, and/or grows; an elegy is a term for a poem which mourns the dead. Picaresque refers to a novel about the misadventures of a roguish protagonist; epistolary refers to a novel written in the form of letters/telegrams/other correspondence (a). Fictional novels can be historical, i.e., based on actual events and characters in history, or speculative, i.e., exploring not actual/current/historical but potential/future events/developments (b). Nonfictional essays can be persuasive, i.e., aiming to convince readers of a position, or expository, i.e., aiming to impart information (c).

21

8. C: Poems are typically the most condensed or economical in their use of words. Plays (a), typically more condensed in language than novels because more of the story is told directly through actions which novels must verbally describe, are still not as condensed as poems because they contain more dialogue. Novels (b) are full-length books, by definition longer than short stories, novelettes, or novellas; they often elaborate more about plot and character development than many poems, thus using more words. They also more often use complete sentences throughout, whereas poems may use phrases in addition to/instead of sentences. Essays (d) tend to expound on nonfictional topics in prose; hence, although they are far shorter than novels, they use many more words to express ideas than plays or most poems.

9. C only: "An Essay on the Shaking Palsy" by James Parkinson, M.D., is an 1817 medical work first defining Parkinson's disease, named after him for identifying it. Its five chapters total fewer than 60 pages. (a) and (b) are both actually long poems by eighteenth-century poet/satirist and essayist Alexander Pope. (d) is a 1798 book by economist Thomas R. Malthus (revised editions 1803–1826). (e) is Enlightenment philosopher John Locke's 1689 (dated 1690) empiricist book in four "books" or sections.

10. B: Characters are always found in drama; they are also found in most fictional short stories and novels, and they are sometimes found in poems. Conflict (c) and action (d) are dramatic elements found not only in plays, but also frequently in short stories, novels, and poetry. Narrative (b) is typically found in novels and short stories; some poems also contain narratives (e.g., Longfellow's *The Song of Hiawatha*, Byron's *Childe Harold's Pilgrimage,* etc.). Although some plays include a narrator who periodically provides summaries, transitions, and/or commentaries, plays generally are LESS likely to contain narrative because the characters' actions tell the story.

11. A: In satire, authors ridicule human failings, including unethical behaviors; in realism, authors often pose ethical dilemmas for their characters to confront and resolve. Behaviors are often exaggerated (b) only in satire, to make fun of and/or attack them; in realism, behaviors are depicted as closely to real-life human behaviors as possible. Straightforward, everyday (vernacular) language used by real, ordinary people is used (c) in realism; in satire, authors may use a variety of language to achieve desired effects of sarcasm, irony, and humor through understatement, overstatement, etc. Exposing human vices and foolishness is more important than accuracy in satire; verisimilitude (representing reality accurately) is more important in realism (d).

12. B: Early ballad themes included jealousy, betrayal, murder, war, famine, poverty, etc. as well as love; early sonnet themes included politics, social standing, satire, etc. as well as love. Both genres have prominently featured expressions of love. The sonnet has five main kinds (a): the Petrarchan/Italian, Occitan, Shakespearean/English, Spenserian, and Modern; the ballad has developed many more variations in form. Originally the ballad was often set to music, and it was later associated with operas and musicals; the sonnet originated in dramatic plays and medieval courts. Though some sonnets have been set to music, the sonnet did not originate with music (c). The standard ballad meter is iambic heptameter, albeit with variations; the standard sonnet meter is iambic pentameter (d).

13. D: Historical fiction is set during some previous period of our history, which may be remote, recent, or anything in between; science fiction is set during the possible future (a) or during an imagined alternative present—either one with scientific, social, and other developments not part of current reality. Historical fiction is based on periods, events, and facts from history; science fiction is based on speculations (b) of what may occur through extending current science. However, both forms can be concerned with events occurring around and/or to the characters and inventions (real and/or imaginary) could also be included in either one (c).

14. A: Biography and autobiography share a common type of content: the life story of a real person. But they differ in authorship: biography is written by someone other than the subject, whereas autobiography is written about the author's own life. Persuasive and informational (b) nonfiction differ in content: the former seeks to influence readers, and the latter seeks to provide/explain facts objectively. Informational and biographical (c) nonfiction differ in content: the former imparts information about some subject, and the latter imparts information about someone's life. Autobiography tells the writer's life story, whereas persuasive nonfiction seeks to convince readers of something (d).

15. B: Realistic authors strive to represent reality as closely as possible, even in fiction: they avoid exaggeration, which satire often employs to ridicule social behaviors. Both genres may be written in a serious tone (a) compatible with realism but also useful in satire: Jonathan Swift intensifies the satirical effects of *A Modest Proposal* by making absurd and even horrific recommendations in an ostensibly serious tone. Realists may depict situational irony, e.g., O. Henry in "The Gift of the Magi"; irony is a key satirists' tool. Writing dialogue in the vernacular (d) is a realistic technique equally appropriate in satire.

16. B: Miss Havisham uses Estella, not vice versa (a), by raising her to break men's hearts to gain revenge against men for her fiancé having left her at the altar. Estella in turn marries Drummle to get revenge on Miss Havisham (b) for using her. Magwitch uses Pip by raising Pip's social status to get revenge against society, not Pip (c), for discriminating against Magwitch in court on the basis of social class. Orlick wants revenge against Pip, not vice versa (d), for a series of wrongs he feels Pip committed and for Pip's privileged life, which Orlick envies.

17. D: Choice (a) uses only literal meaning by describing the willow's appearance factually: it has branches that are long and that trail. Choice (b) uses figurative meaning with a simile that explicitly compares the willow's leaves to teardrops in appearance. Choice (c) also uses figurative language with a metaphor that implies comparison by describing the willow as weeping into the stream, as well as anthropomorphism by giving human qualities to the non-human willow.

18. D: In *Sherlock Holmes* (a), the first-person narrative is told by Dr. Watson, a close friend of main character Sherlock Holmes, but not the main character. In *The Tell-Tale Heart* (b) and *Gulliver's Travels* (c), the main characters are also the narrators, and they speak in the first person ("I," "me," etc.).

19. B: Throughout history, teenagers have fallen in love; moreover, in Shakespeare's time when people did not live as long as today, serious love in adolescence was not necessarily even age-inappropriate. Thus Shakespeare does not attribute the tragedy to the characters' youth in this play (a). One theme in this play is the relationship of love and violence (c), with love often causing violence. Another theme is that of fate, which does control the characters (d) in this play, emphasized in the Chorus's first speech describing them as "star-crossed."

20. B, D, and E: In the quoted verse, Alfred Tennyson uses imagery (b), describing the eagle using wording that evokes sensory impressions for readers, i.e., visual details of its appearance and tactile details of its behavior; alliteration (d), repeating the same sounds across the words *clasps*, *crag*, and *crooked*—the hard /k/ sound complements and reinforces the imagery; and personification (e), giving an animal human qualities by calling the eagle "he" and its talons "hands." This verse does NOT include simile (a), i.e., explicit comparison; or metaphor (c), i.e., implicit comparison.

21. A: Students must be able to connect informational text they read with their existing knowledge and draw inferences from it in order to not only comprehend the material alone (b), but also to make conclusions AND critical judgments about it (c), as well as their own interpretations of it (d).

22. A: In situational irony, things are revealed as other than they seem to both characters and readers, such as when Dickens makes Miss Havisham appear to be Pip's benefactor, only to reveal ultimately that it is really Magwitch. In verbal irony, a character (or narrator) says one thing but means another, such as when Poe has Montresor agree with Fortunato's literal statement that he will not die of a cough; ultimately, readers discover Montresor's true meaning: the cough will not kill Fortunato because Montresor will (b). In dramatic irony, a character knows less than the readers/audience, like Romeo (c). Therefore, (d) is incorrect.

23. C: The meaning of this opening sentence is primarily literal: it establishes who the main character is, what he does, and his current situation. While this novella contains some symbols, the opening sentence is not symbolic (a) of anything particular. The meaning is not implicit (b) but explicit. (Hemingway was known for the clear, direct simplicity of his writing style.) The sentence is not true (d) because this book is a work of fiction.

24. B: The reader can infer that Mamzelle Aurélie was independent from the description of her never having thought of marrying, never having been in love, having declined a proposal, and so far never having lived to regret this. Readers cannot infer *from this passage alone* that she was lonesome (a), was changing her mind (c), or was sorry she was unmarried (d). Readers may infer from the *title* she ultimately regrets something in this story, but not from this passage alone.

25. C: According to the first paragraph, it is not a certain number of absences (a)—no numbers are identified there—that distinguishes chronic absence from truancy. Whereas truancy is defined as many sequential days of unexcused absences, chronic absence is defined as nonsequential days of excused OR unexcused absences, so whether they are excused or not does not differentiate chronic absence from truancy (b). The difference is defined as sequential versus nonsequential absence days (c); therefore, (d) is incorrect.

26. C: The second paragraph cites a national statistic of the estimated annual number of chronically absent students; plus it offers a statistic of the proportion this represents for some states. Therefore, (a) is incorrect. The first paragraph (b) identifies academic and social benefits students miss through absence, and differentially defines truancy versus chronic absence, but it does not cite any statistics. The third paragraph (d) gives general examples of the impacts of chronic absence, but it gives no supporting statistics.

27. B: The statistics (a) given in the second paragraph do not support the statement referenced; they precede it, supporting the first paragraph's definition of chronic absence and its reality in numbers. The author supports her statement in the third paragraph's opening sentence by following with a generalized example of how cumulative absences negatively affect current and future student achievement and success. Therefore, (c) is incorrect. The differential definition (d) given in the first paragraph establishes what chronic absence is; it does not support the third paragraph's statement.

28. D: By having the main character narrate in the first person, Poe emphasizes his divorce from reality: he repeatedly insists he is not crazy, simultaneously demonstrating he is by describing his abnormal obsession, paranoid delusions, oblivion to normal cues like noises that would alert neighbors, and gloating over his brilliance in committing the perfect crime even though he has already betrayed his guilt to police. Readers do not identify with (a) or feel more sympathetic (b) toward him; if anything, they feel more detached from him through his speaking for himself than if a sane, third-person narrator told his story. His firsthand account does not lend him credibility (c): Poe deliberately uses the first-person narrative point of view to illuminate the character's madness through his speech.

29. C: Though the first clause of this sentence has been widely maligned, ridiculed, parodied and praised, imitated, and even made the basis of literary contests for both bad and good writing, it and the rest of the sentence do establish the setting such that it contributes greatly to mood, i.e., the emotions it evokes in readers. It does not contribute to plot (a) because it includes no actions or events yet. It does not contribute to tone (b), which reflects the attitude of the author rather than evoking an attitude in the reader. It does not contribute to conflict (d) in the same way it does not contribute to plot.

30. D: The arguably most descriptive words in this sentence are adjectives: dark, stormy, violent, scanty. Bulwer-Lytton also used verbs (a), i.e., fell, was checked, swept, rattling, agitating, struggled; although the last four of these are descriptive, they are arguably not as descriptive as the adjectives. He used some descriptive nouns (b) as well: night, rain, gust, wind, darkness; yet these are still not as evocative as the adjectives. Of adverbs (c), "fiercely" is certainly descriptive, but it is the only one.

31. B: This poem is a classic example of extended metaphor, an implied comparison that extends across the entire work, here of America's Union ("state") as being like a sailing ship braving the treacherous waters of governance. A single metaphor (a) is an isolated incidence of such an implied comparison within a work rather than one encompassing the whole work. A simile (c) is a direct/explicit comparison, e.g., "The state is *like* a ship." The poem does contain auditory, visual, and tactile imagery (d), but extended metaphor is the most prominent literary device of the poem overall.

32. C: This poem is written in iambic ($\cup$ / = one unstressed syllable, then one stressed) tetrameter (four beats per line). Iambic pentameter (a), with five iambic beats per line, is the most common meter in English verse; all of Shakespeare's verses use it. A specific example is Theodore Roethke's villanelle, "The Waking." An example of anapestic ($\cup\cup$ / = two unstressed syllables, then one stressed) tetrameter (b) is George Gordon, Lord Byron's "The Destruction of Sennacherib." Dactylic (/$\cup\cup$ = one stressed, two unstressed syllables) dimeter (two beats per line) (d) is used by Alfred, Lord Tennyson in "The Charge of the Light Brigade."

33. A: The very regular rhyme and meter in this poem reinforce the idea of the ship of state as strong and forging steadily onward despite all perils. Therefore, these are not uneven, and the poem does not have a theme of insecurity (b). Though regular, the rhyme and meter are not monotonous, and Longfellow meant to convey a sense that the ship of state was steadfast, brave, and dependable/worthy of the people's faith and hope, not unchanging (c). The regular rhyme and meter are even, not choppy; although Longfellow describes a stormy sea as part of the extended metaphor, he does not mirror it in sound or rhythm (d).

34. B: That our ancestors created a new nation would go under the main ideas column in the two-column notes active reading strategy, as this is the central idea of the first sentence and paragraph in the speech. Choice (a) would go under the details column as it identifies the time of the main idea. Choices (c) and (d) would also go under the details column as they are each modifiers identifying characteristics of the main idea (how it was conceived and to what it was dedicated).

35. D: Comparing ideas or elements (a) shows their similarities, as does making analogies (b) between them. Contrasting ideas or elements (c) shows their differences. Grouping ideas or elements into categories (d) can show both similarities and differences—similarities among those grouped together in the same category, and differences among the separate categories and their members.

36. C, D, and E: In a book of informational text, both a glossary and an index list their entries in alphabetical order (a), and both are typically found at the back of the book (b). Only an index lists the book's main or most important topics (c), and references all page numbers where they are found (d). Only a glossary lists new or technical vocabulary or terminology used in the book and provides definitions of the terms (e) it lists.

37. D: Sentences (a) and (b) use "smart" to indicate the connotation (i.e., implied or inferred meaning) of rude, disrespectful, etc., which readers can determine from sentence context. Sentence (c) uses "smart" for its denotation (i.e., its definition or literal meaning) of showing intelligence, thinking well, behaving sensibly, using good judgment, acting strategically, etc.

38. B and C: Technical language in scientific text should achieve a balance between grandiose (a) and self-deprecating (d) mood, as neither extreme is acceptable (e.g., "Our findings are insignificant" is too self-deprecating, while "Our findings are indisputable" is too grandiose). It should be more impersonal (b) and professional (c) than vernacular or literary language. It should not *always* use passive voice (e), which makes tone more impersonal and avoids first person. Science professors traditionally advocated a passive voice, but today's science editors find it dull and weak, so science writers may alternate active and passive voices.

39. B: Authors of informational texts do explicitly state their point of view and/or purpose sometimes, but NOT always (a); many authors do not overtly identify it, so readers must infer it (b), which is easier when the author's position is more opinionated, but harder when it is neutral or balanced (c)—or when the text itself is difficult. Therefore, readers have to analyze some text to identify author point of view or purpose, which they should NOT assume indicates poor writing (d).

40. A: An allusion is a reference to something or someone well-known that adds symbolism and/or resonance. A paradox (b) is a seemingly contradictory statement which nevertheless is true. An analogy (c) is a comparison of two different things that share some common elements. A parody (d) is a kind of satire that ridicules a work's subject and/or style through imitation.

41. B: Shakespeare used the connotative meanings of the words to create a metaphor, wherein the stage, players, exits and entrances, and parts played symbolize the world, people, and roles or stages in life. Therefore, his meaning is NOT primarily denotative (a), i.e., focusing on the literal word definitions; nor is it half denotative and half connotative (c). The words must have one or the other type of meaning, not neither (d): text authors use words literally or figuratively or both.

42. D: Anticipating objections (a), arguing to refute them, and depicting them as weak support author views by bringing objections up before readers can raise or even think of them. Citing expert opinions (b) supports author views by showing readers that *a knowledgeable authority on the subject* agrees. Bandwagon appeals (c) support author views by showing readers *everybody else* agrees. Testimonials (d)—anecdotes or especially quotations—support author views by showing readers *others* agree (not necessarily an authority or everybody).

43. C: Authors who normally write informational text using technical language may have to write using non-technical language for a number of reasons, including for communicating simpler, clearer messages rather than denser content (a); informing colleagues in other fields as well as their own (b); procuring funding or support for budgets and/or projects (c); and to inform a wide range of citizens of important information they have a right to receive, even without having knowledge (d) of subject-specific jargon, terminology, or vocabulary.

44. B: Readers should first identify the conclusion of an argument, and then identify the premises the author gives to support that conclusion—not vice versa (a). However, readers should then list the premises first, followed by the conclusion, rather than listing them in the order of identification (c). They should try to paraphrase the premises, not only to clarify them, but also to make them fit together with the conclusion (d).

45. A: When readers consider why an author wrote an informational text, determining author purpose gives them greater insights to the text, develops their critical reading skills (b), enables readers to know what to expect from the text (c), and enables readers to respond more effectively to the text's purpose and persuasion (d).

46. C: The part of speech that names a person, place, or thing (a) is a noun. The part of speech that names an action or state of being (b) is a verb. An adverb is the part of speech that modifies (describes) a verb, adjective, or another adverb (c). The part of speech that modifies and describes a noun or (another) adjective (d) is an adjective.

47. D: Repetition—of the same words, phrases, clauses, sounds, images, etc. within one advertisement; and repetition of the same advertising message—are both effective tools of persuasion, as are sentimental appeals. Advertising uses humor to persuade more often than news or advocacy (a). "Weasel words" that qualify whatever they modify often accompany overstated claims (b). Using hyperbole, superlatives, and other intensifiers can also be highly persuasive (c).

48. B: Satire is a genre of writing that may be used in informational as well as literary (and informational literary) texts to ridicule human and social faults through various indirect devices, including irony (a), i.e., saying the opposite of what one means; overstatement (c), i.e., exaggerating; and/or understatement (d), i.e., minimizing the importance or seriousness of something in describing it.

49. B: Adjectives (a) modify nouns or pronouns by describing them, e.g., *white* is an adjective describing and modifying the noun *house.* Adverbs (b) modify verbs, adjectives, or other adverbs—everything *except* nouns or pronouns. Adverbs answer the questions *how, when,* or *where,* e.g., *slowly, later,* or *downstairs.* Nouns (c) are words that name a person, place, or thing, e.g., *girl, city,* or *house.* They do not modify other parts of speech. They are typically subjects or objects in sentences, clauses, or phrases. Verbs (d) identify actions or states of being, e.g., *to run, to smile, to feel,* or *to be.* Like verbs, they do not modify other words. They are typically predicates in sentences, clauses, or phrases. *To be* can also be a linking verb (copula).

50. C: This is an example of a dangling participle. The participle *completing* was done by Peter, but the sentence construction makes it seem as if the teacher did it. This makes no sense: the teacher would not give Peter a high grade after completing the assignment correctly. It can be corrected to "After Peter completed the assignment correctly, the teacher gave him a high grade" or "After completing the assignment correctly, Peter received a high grade from the teacher."

51. B: A semicolon is used to punctuate between two independent clauses, as in the sentence given. It is also used in sentences that contain additional internal punctuation, which this sentence also has. (a) is incorrect because it contains a comma splice, i.e., two independent clauses joined by a comma without a coordinating conjunction (such as "and" or "but"). (c) is not as correct because it separates two related clauses with a period; joining them with a semicolon reinforces their connection. Choice (d) incorrectly uses a semicolon together with the coordinating conjunction "and." With a coordinating conjunction between independent clauses, a comma should be used rather than a semicolon.

52. C: However is a conjunctive adverb (adverb used like a conjunction) connecting independent clauses. A preposition (a) connects nouns, pronouns, noun phrases, and pronoun phrases to other words; in this sentence, to and with are prepositions. A conjunction (b) like and, but, or, nor, etc. connects words, phrases, and clauses. For example, in the rewritten sentence, "I would like to go with you, but I won't have time," but is a conjunction—specifically a coordinating conjunction, connecting independent clauses. A subordinating conjunction (d) introduces a dependent or subordinate clause, connecting it to an independent clause, e.g., "I cannot go with you because I won't have time."

53. A: "Although Ted had an impressive education" is a dependent or subordinate clause, introduced by the subordinating conjunction "Although" and modifying the independent clause "he had little experience working with individuals." The second dependent clause is the relative clause "which made him less effective at relating to them," introduced by the relative pronoun "which" and modifying "he had little experience." Hence there is not just one dependent clause (b), (d), or none (c), nor are there two independent clauses (b), (c).

54. B: A simple (a) sentence is one independent clause. This sentence has a dependent clause ("Every time they visited") and an independent clause ("she got to know him a little bit better.") This defines a complex (b) sentence. A compound (c) sentence includes two independent clauses but no dependent clause. A compound-complex (d) sentence includes two independent clauses and one or more dependent clauses.

55. A: Despite its length, this is a simple sentence—one independent clause, including a compound predicate (entered, walked, sat) modifying the subject (man) and a participial phrase (wearing) with multiple objects (raincoat, hat, shoe). All modifiers are adjectives (tall, black, yellow, red, smallest, other), adverbs (down, alone, farthest), prepositions (away from), prepositional phrases (to the back, at the smallest table, from the staff), and the participial phrase (wearing a black raincoat). It is not complex (b), having no dependent r subordinate clause; not compound (c), having only one independent clause; and not compound-complex (d), having only one independent and no dependent clause.

56. B: The topics of cooperative projects and/or discussions and whether they are age-appropriate in difficulty relate most to cognitive developmental levels, i.e., what they can understand. Social developmental levels (a) relate to whether students can interact effectively in peer groups. Emotional developmental levels (c) relate to student emotional intelligence, i.e., emotional self-management plus sensitivity to, understanding of, and appropriate response to others' emotions. Behavioral developmental levels (d) relate to whether students can regulate their behaviors appropriately within peer groups.

57. D: The suffix –ation (a) commonly forms nouns from verbs, e.g., *converse* and *conversation, confront* and *confrontation, revoke* and *revocation, celebrate* and *celebration*, etc. The suffix –ness (b) commonly forms nouns from adjectives, e.g., *happy* and *happiness, kind* and *kindness, dark* and *darkness*, etc.; as does the suffix –ity (c), e.g., *formal* and *formality, sensitive* and *sensitivity, gay* and *gaiety*, etc. However, the suffix –id (d) commonly forms adjectives from nouns, e.g., *candor* and *candid, livor* and *livid, rabies* and *rabid, rigor* and *rigid*, etc.

58. A: A glossary is a list of specific vocabulary or terminology used in a text with definitions for each word listed. This is the best reference source to find the meanings of technical or subject-specific words used in the text. A dictionary (b) gives the spelling, pronunciation, syllabication, definition, and sometimes examples used in sentences of ALL recognized words in the written language. A style manual (c) tells writers how to organize written works, cite references, etc. A spell checker (d), commonly included in word-processing programs, identifies misspelled or mistyped words in documents.

59. A: This sentence contains a misplaced modifier: "not only" modifies "a decline," and "but also" modifies "common sense." This is illogical because "not only" and "but also" are logically connected and thus should both modify the objects of the preposition "in," which in turn modify the noun "decline." To be correct, it should be written either as "not only a decline in manners, but also a decline in common sense" or as "a decline not only in manners, but also in common sense." This is not a squinting modifier (b), which makes the meaning unclear by potentially modifying either of two words, e.g., "Children who smile seldom are sad," which could mean children who rarely smile are sad, or children who smile are rarely sad. It is not a dangling participle (c), e.g., "While growing up, Popsicles were popular," wherein the participle is left dangling without a subject: the Popsicles were not growing up. It should be something like, "While growing up, we liked Popsicles" or "While I was growing up, Popsicles were popular." Because (a) is correct, (d) is incorrect.

60. D: This is a simple sentence despite its length. It has only one independent clause, which contains a single subject (He) and a compound predicate with multiple verbs (woke, looked, got, ate, got, drove, parked, walked, opened, went). All other parts are prepositions, prepositional phrases, adjectives, adverbs, and articles modifying verbs and nouns. The other types all include more than one clause—either more than one independent plus at least one dependent clause (a), more than one independent clause (b), or an independent and a dependent clause (c).

61. A: A complex sentence combines independent and dependent clauses. The first clause is independent, the second ("although…") is dependent as it cannot stand alone as a sentence. Choice (b) is a compound sentence, i.e., two independent clauses joined by a coordinating conjunction. Choice (c) is a simple sentence, i.e., a single independent clause. Choice (d) is a compound–complex sentence, i.e., two independent clauses joined by coordinating conjunction ("and"), followed by a dependent ("if …") clause.

62. B: This is a compound sentence, i.e., two independent clauses joined by a conjunctive adverb ("unfortunately"). It is not a simple sentence (a) because it has two independent clauses; a simple sentence would have only one. It is not a complex sentence (c) because it has no dependent clauses; a complex sentence has at least one independent and one dependent clause. It is not a compound–complex (d) sentence because it has no dependent clause; a compound–complex sentence has at least two independent clauses and at least one dependent clause.

63. B: This is a compound–complex sentence because it includes a dependent clause ("After David met Marcia"), which cannot stand on its own as a sentence but depends on an independent clause, plus two independent clauses ("he knew she was the one" and "he soon proposed marriage to her") joined by a coordinating conjunction ("and"). A compound sentence (a) has two independent clauses but no dependent clause. A complex sentence (c) has at least one dependent clause and only one independent clause, not two. A simple sentence (d) has only one independent clause and no dependent clauses.

64. A: From the syntax of this sentence, the reader can determine which parts of speech the missing words must be: the first blank must be filled by a noun, the second by a verb. However, the reader cannot determine from syntax which specific noun or verb these should be (b). The noun must be a thing, place, or event, but this encompasses a great many words (e.g., building, site, meeting, party, riot, class, school, company, etc.). The verb must be transitive because it takes an object ("what happened"), but this also includes myriad verbs (e.g., see, observe, find out, discover, report, address, change, correct, imitate, avoid, etc.). Therefore, answers (c) and (d) are incorrect.

65. A: *Retro-* is Latin meaning backward or behind. Retroactive means acting backward, i.e., upon earlier events (e.g., "Monthly fees will be refunded retroactively to your first payment"). Retrograde refers to moving backward, e.g., planets in astronomy; deteriorating/degenerating in biology, or generally in reverse order or receding. Retrospect/retrospective mean looking backward on previous events. A retrovirus (e.g., the AIDS virus) enables reversing genetic transcription to be RNA-to-DNA to produce new RNA retroviruses by incorporating viral DNA into the host's DNA, instead of typical DNA-to-RNA transcription. Retro-rockets decelerate or separate stages of larger rockets to which they are attached by aiming exhaust toward instead of away from flight direction, i.e., backward. "Retro" fashions are inspired by earlier styles. By knowing the meaning of at least one of these words, the student can determine the meaning of the prefix, and thus of the other words.

66. D: The student has used the same adjective, "wonderful," four times in the same sentence to modify four different nouns. To give her description more variety, she should consult an online thesaurus to find synonyms (e.g., terrific, great, outstanding, exemplary, etc.). A grammar guide (a) will not offer vocabulary synonyms, and the student's sentence has no grammatical issues. An encyclopedia (b) offers information on many subjects, but not word synonyms. An online dictionary (c) will provide a few to several synonyms for "wonderful," but a thesaurus will offer many more.

67. D: The argumentative mode of writing has the purpose of convincing readers to agree with the author's belief or opinion about a chosen issue. The narrative (a) mode has the purpose of telling readers a story. The telling may include sharing an insight or revelation that the author or character(s) gained through the story's experiences and/or something they learned through them. The informative (b) mode has the purpose of sharing information with readers, to tell them something they did not know, and/or how to do something. The explanatory (c) mode shares information with readers and also analyzes, illuminates, or illustrates it for the purpose of helping them understand it.

68. D: Introducing readers to new information (a), explaining to readers how a process functions (b), and developing a concept for readers (c) are all primary functions of informative or explanatory writing. Proving a point to convince readers (d) to believe or agree with the author's position is a primary function of argumentative writing. The former means to inform, the latter to persuade.

69. C: Although many people keep private journals to confide and/or process their personal experiences (a) and emotions—in which cases they need not be concerned about their writing mechanics, as only they will ever see them (b)—in other cases, authors write journals they expect or hope to publish someday (c); these do require attention to mechanics and editing. Some authors also write journals for their therapeutic benefits (d).

70. D: An essay's introduction should answer three questions: the subject of the essay (a), how the essay addresses the subject (b), and what the essay will prove (d)—which is the essay's thesis statement. To answer how the essay addresses the subject (b), readers should identify how the author organized the essay (c) through a brief summary of its main points and the evidence offered to support them.

71. C: When writing an essay, experts advise using one paragraph to introduce one main point, present evidence supporting that point, and explain how these relate to the thesis. Each additional main point, its supporting evidence, and their relation to the thesis should occupy a separate paragraph. All main points, accompanying evidence, and their relation to the thesis should NOT be in one long paragraph (a). Neither should writers separate each point, supporting evidence, and relationship to the thesis into different paragraphs (b). Because option (c) is the general rule, option (d) is incorrect.

72. D: For writing, teachers should instruct their students to think about what kinds of proof and/or evidence they will need to provide for their readers to agree with their points (a). They should instruct students to consider not only what points they will make in writing that their readers might agree with, but moreover what points their readers are likely to disagree with (b), and how to refute or counter those disagreements to persuade skeptical audiences. Teachers should have students think about what information their readers already know and what information they will share with their readers (c). They should additionally instruct students to consider what information they and their readers share in common (d).

73. D: Outlines benefit students (a) and professional writers (b), not only one or the other. The main point(s) of a paragraph or an entire piece, and the details that support the main point(s), can be more quickly identified in outlines that summarize them in single sentences than they can by reading through all the additional language of a fully developed piece. Outlines can be used not only to plan writing (c), but also to analyze existing writing (d). Readers (or writers reviewing their own work) can make outlines to summarize the main point/idea in one sentence, and then list and number the supporting details, also each in a single sentence.

74. C: Focusing each paragraph on one main idea (a) contributes to writing good paragraphs. The writer may state this idea overtly in a topic sentence, or simply imply a more obvious main topic that readers can infer. Giving specific details to develop that main idea (b) is also a practice that results in better paragraphs. However, it is not true that the more details, the better (c): excessive details will destroy the paragraph's focus and confuse readers. Another practice for developing good paragraphs is using specific structural patterns (d), e.g., comparison–contrast, division and classification, analogy, cause-and-effect, definition, description, narration, process, or example and illustration.

75. B: Parallelism refers to parallel structure, i.e., maintaining the same grammatical construction among like and related words or phrases. For example, "He likes to hike, climb mountains, and ride bicycles" uses parallelism by keeping all of the verbs in the infinitive; "He likes to hike, climb mountains, and riding bicycles" lacks parallelism because the first two verbs are infinitives but the third is a participle/gerund. Repetition (a) lends coherence by connecting a paragraph's sentence through repeating its important words, phrases, and their referents (e.g., pronouns). Transitions (c) give coherence by using words and phrases to connect sentences to one another. Consistency (d) provides coherence by maintaining the same tone, point of view, and language register throughout the paragraph and the whole piece.

76. A: Essays with good organization have many benefits, including being more likely to win reader acceptance of the validity of their theses; being more likely to hold reader attention (b); and both being easier for writers to compose, and giving readers better guides for following as they read them (c), (d).

77. B: Readers of reputable newspapers have been accustomed to expecting quality in content, and they usually transfer this expectation to blogs (a). Readers also expect easily readable layouts in print and online alike. However, reading onscreen is harder than on paper, so legibility becomes even more important (b). Also, because readers cannot skim online articles as they do in print (d), but instead must scroll down, blogs require *more* complexity to format and write than newspapers (c), as well as subheadings, graphics, and other text features predicting (b) what follows.

78. D: The purpose of narrative (a) writing is storytelling. Even when authors want to afford insights and/or teach lessons as well as entertain readers, they accomplish their purposes through storytelling. The purposes of expository (b) writing are to inform, explain, and/or direct readers. The purpose of persuasive (c) writing is to convince readers to believe or agree with the author's position and/or argument. The purpose of speculative (d) writing is to encourage readers to explore ideas and potential responses rather than entertain, tell stories, inform, explain, direct, or convince.

79. D: When older students use simpler vocabulary and syntax, and printing instead of script (a), this is an example of writing for certain audiences. When word choice and diction stimulate readers to feel empathy and/or sympathy (b), or to question or challenge opposing viewpoints (c), these are both examples of certain occasions for writing. Writers selecting certain formats, e.g., exposition, persuasion, narration, etc., and kinds of language (d) is an example of writing for certain purposes.

80. C: Publisher name and publication city (a) must be cited for both print and electronic books. For both print and electronic articles, the periodical name and volume, issue, and page numbers (b) must be cited. The database name, database publisher name, and URL (d) are included only when citing electronic sources because these do not apply to print media.

81. B: When students quote others' writing in their research papers, one general principle is if they cannot write the same number of words as/more than in the quotation to analyze, explain, refute, or support that quotation, they are most likely using the quotation as padding to make their papers longer. Another way students often pad papers is by following a quotation with a summary of what it means, which is inadvisable (c) because summarizing it is not as engaging or original intellectually as analyzing, synthesizing, and/or evaluating it (d). It is not true that parenthetically identifying other related studies within a sentence interrupts one's argument (a); this is actually a good technique for incorporating others' work that agrees/disagrees with one's position without disrupting the flow of the writing.

82. B, C, and D: Speechmakers are advised not to be formal (a) or theatrical (e) in their presentation, but rather to be more natural (d) as they would behave in a normal conversation. This makes audiences more comfortable and enables them to relate better to the speaker and the speech. Speakers should also be confident (c), which will support effective speech delivery better than being obviously ill at ease. To establish rapport with the audience, speakers can connect personally with them by being direct (b).

83. A: Experts do advise communications presenters to combine two or three types of media for the most effectiveness, rather than limiting themselves to only one (b). The presenter's budget will also necessarily influence their choice of media (c). For example, TV is more expensive than radio; radio is more expensive than paying a PR writer for print communications; and some presenters can produce their own news releases and photos at no additional cost. How long a communication is will affect the media choice (d), e.g., in terms of costs and of maintaining audience attention, etc.

84. A: When a speaker is making a statement or answering a question from the audience, s/he should not take three or more minutes to get to the point, which will lose listener attention. Getting off the subject has the same effect. However, speakers should not be afraid to pause before answering audience questions (b): this gives them time to formulate a clear response, as well as demonstrating to their listeners that they are thoughtful and in control. Including too many anecdotes and details (c) is not good: it causes audiences to lose track of the subject/get confused. Similarly, speakers should include necessary information but not all other interesting information. (d): Information overload triggers listeners' brains to shut down due to having more input than they can process.

85. B: Despite that the question is repeated often, this method of appeal is not best identified as repetition (a), but as slogan use. (b): The question which the ads have made familiar is an example of a company/brand's slogan. Slogans are catchphrases that advertisers want consumers to remember and associate with their brands. A bandwagon (c) appeal advises using a brand because everybody else does, i.e., through popularity/peer pressure. A testimonial (d) is a statement endorsing/supporting a brand by a celebrity/well-known individual/other consumer.

86. A = 6, B = 5, C = 4, D = 1, E = 3, F = 2: The song repeating one of the brand name's two words (a) over and over appeals to audiences through repetition. Using words that lack specific meaning but sound good (b), e.g., "best," "tasty," "healthy," "amazing," "smooth and silky," etc., are known as glittering generalities (5). Displaying a brand/product with an American flag (c) appeals by transfer/association (4) of the brand/product with patriotism. Contrasting two brands via a checklist (d), typically with the advertised brand having all features listed against a competing brand having few/none, is a product comparison (1). Showing people in desirable interactions/situations (e) appeals to emotion (3): viewers expect to feel the same by using the product. Citing statistics supporting product efficacy (f) appeals to reason (2).

87. D: Tracing and evaluating arguments and specific claims in a text are shared standards for grades 6 and 7, and delineating and evaluating arguments and specific claims in a text is a standard for grade 8 (a). Distinguishing whether claims are supported by evidence and reasons or not (b) is a part of the standard for grade 6 only. Assessing whether the reasoning in claims is sound and the evidence is relevant and sufficient to support the claims (c) is a part of the standards for grades 7 and 8. Recognizing whether irrelevant evidence has been introduced (d) is a part of the standard for grade 8 only.

88. A = 4: Post hoc ergo propter hoc means after this, therefore because of this. This fallacy assumes that sequence equals causation, i.e., A caused B just because B followed A. b = 1: A straw man fallacy argues against an exaggeration or caricature of someone's argument instead of the real argument. c = 2: Ad hominem means against the man, i.e., arguing against the person making the argument instead of against the argument's validity. d = 3: A non sequitur (Latin for "it does not follow") states a conclusion that does not logically follow the preceding premise. In this example, a missing step is needed, e.g., "Affirmative action will decrease racism."

89. B: When assessing the relevance of any argument, it is important to remember that relevance is a matter of degree, not an either/or or yes/no proposition. In this example, the salesperson's argument for buying the car because of its great paint job is *less* relevant than the transmission's condition (a), which is more important in a good vehicle. The paint job is less relevant than a bent frame (b), which negatively affects the car's function and value; or how well the engine runs (c), which affects functioning far more than the paint job. However, the paint job is not completely irrelevant (d): most customers want good-looking used cars.

90. C: When students write for their classmates, they should use language that is more informal and age-appropriate, not more sophisticated (a). When requesting additional privileges from parents, students should use language that is not simpler (b) but more sophisticated. When writing for younger children, students should use more vivid and entertaining language (c), including some humor when appropriate. When asking parental permission for more independent activities, students should use language that seems more mature and serious rather than using humor (d).

91. C: Sentences (a), (b), and (d) are examples of information that goes off the point by not supporting the main idea, as none of these indicate a lack of canine intelligence. However, sentence (c) is an example of evidence supporting the main point because it illustrates it by stating the dog does not respond to his name, implying he has not learned to recognize it in five years.

92. B: English language learners (ELLs) generally benefit from contextual learning of vocabulary because it helps to solidify the meaning and usage of the newly-learned words. Both vocabulary in isolation (a) and vocabulary in volume (b) typically refer to rote memorization, which does not provide the retention benefits or provide the student with contextual experience. Answer (d) is wrong because speech proficiency levels do not necessarily correspond to a student's reading and vocabulary skills.

93. D: When students are unfamiliar with group discussions, teachers should not introduce these by beginning with topics below student age level (a); such topics will bore students and fail to engage them. Neither should teachers assign group discussion topics above student age levels (b), which will confuse, lose, and/or overwhelm them. They should take student cognitive, emotional, behavioral, and social levels of development into account when choosing discussion topics. For all students, and especially those inexperienced with discussion groups, teachers should explain *and* model appropriate behaviors—not just explain (c)—before beginning a discussion. These behaviors include eye contact and confirming and restating others' messages.

94. D: In the structural paragraph pattern of division (a), a whole is separated into its components by some principle (e.g., steps, body parts, etc.). In narration (b), the paragraph relates a story or part of one, e.g., an anecdote supporting its main idea. In definition (c), the paragraph defines a centrally important term in detail. In description (d), the writer uses specific details, including sensory, in the paragraph to show readers instead of telling them about someone or something.

95. B: Coherent written paragraphs have parts that clearly fit together (a) and flow well from one part to another (b); conceptual content that is expressed in structural patterns that are congruent with the concepts, not contrasting (c); and writer control at the sentence level, which does not undermine but promotes paragraph coherence (d).

96. A: In both the fictional narrative genre and the nonfictional informational genre, the author will demonstrate some individual writing style; even very factual and objective expositional writing will reveal some personal stylistic characteristics. Labeled diagrams and photos (B) are more likely to be found in informational nonfiction. The majority of books with excitement and drama (C) are fictional narratives (some informational nonfiction books are presented in narrative form and include excitement, especially in children's literature, but these are the minority). Themes and plots (D) are also literary elements associated with fictional narrative.

97. A: Having sentences unified by integrated, interrelated ideas is a characteristic of a *coherent* written paragraph rather than a *cohesive* one. A cohesive written paragraph has sentences that flow easily from one to another (b); connect old information in one sentence to new information in the next (c); and/or start with old and end with new information, connecting these within one sentence (d).

98. C: A paragraph can be cohesive but not coherent (a) or coherent but not cohesive (b). Hence one does not guarantee the other (d). For example, a paragraph may be cohesive when ideas and words are connected across sentences, yet not coherent when each sentence has a new topic.

34

Alternatively, a paragraph may be coherent when readers can read and understand it, yet not cohesive when sentences are not connected lexically or grammatically.

99. C: To produce writing that is both cohesive and coherent, writers should begin sentences with old or familiar information (a), introducing new information at the end of the sentence or in a new sentence; introduce familiar information by beginning sentences with short, simple phrases (b); make transitions between ideas obvious to readers (c); and maintain consistent topics throughout (d).

100. D: First the writer should narrow down all topics included to a main idea. Then s/he should identify main points supporting that main idea, decide how to sequence those main points, list all the details that support each of the main points, and then organize those details in a chosen sequential order (e.g., by association, by logical progression, from strongest to weakest, or from weakest to strongest).

101. B, C, and E: Teachers should activate students' existing knowledge (b) to prepare them for reading content; help students determine their purposes for reading (c) before they start; and assess existing student vocabulary knowledge, preteach key text vocabulary, and discuss vocabulary in text (e) students will encounter. They can have students construct graphic organizers (a) *during* reading to help them understand concepts. *After* students read, teachers can have them write about the text and discuss their responses to the text (d) in class.

102. C: According to experts, research shows that teachers should explicitly teach their students writing strategies, including prewriting planning, composition, revision, and editing, by first modeling the strategies; then guiding students in practicing them; and then, once they have learned the strategies, letting students practice using them independently. They should not skip the guided practice step (a): students need assistance learning to apply demonstrated strategies before practicing on their own. Students learn better with than without teacher models (b), which must be presented before, not after guided practice (d).

103. B: Studies show that cooperative learning is an effective practice for teaching many things, including writing (a). Experts recommend that when assigning cooperative writing partners or groups, teachers provide students with both a structure (c), and explicit expectations (d) for both partnership/group and individual performance.

104. C: In the process writing approach, elements include having students write for authentic audiences (a), interact with other students throughout the writing process (b), take personal responsibility for their written work (c), and self-evaluate their writing (d).

105. A: Formative assessments typically use informal testing methods, whereas summative assessments typically use formal testing methods. Formative assessments typically are not supported statistically (b) or norm referenced as formal, standardized tests are. Unlike summative assessments, formative assessments are made not after (d) but during instruction, enabling teachers to monitor student progress and adjust ongoing instruction as needed.

106. B: Research finds that the single greatest change in classroom instruction for improving student learning and achievement is feedback, which students and teachers get best from formative assessments. Summative assessments are best for comparison (a) of students to normative student samples, classes to statewide/nationwide classes at the same grade level, and schools to other schools, but they do not give such immediate feedback during ongoing instruction (c). Although they yield more individual student data, formative assessments are typically informal and not standardized and hence are not used to make comparisons (d) the way that standardized summative assessments are.

107. A: Critiques of final projects, e.g., art projects, research projects, music recitals, etc., are examples of summative assessments because they measure student achievement following instruction. Oral question-and-answer sessions (b) are examples of formative assessments because they can be brief, can be administered often, and can be used to monitor ongoing student progress. Running records (c) keep track of student performance in real time (e.g., oral reading fluency) and are also formative assessments. Pop quizzes (d) are typically short, may be given at any time, and cover the most recent information during instruction; thus, they are also examples of formative assessments.

108. C: To get data to inform a school improvement plan (a), a teacher could use a summative assessment, comparing student scores at the end of the school year to their baseline scores obtained at the beginning of that year. This can also be done to show accountability to the federal government (e.g., meeting adequate yearly progress criteria) to get or keep school funding (b); and to get data on student progress toward instructional objectives over the entire school year (d). A teacher would use a formative assessment to get data about individual student performance (c); summative assessments yield more group data and less individual data.

109. C: Strength and closure are important principles for written conclusions. Readers perceive from a strong conclusion that the main points made were meaningful and important (a), and that the evidence supporting those main points was well-developed (d). Readers perceive from a conclusion that achieves closure that the writer said what was needed, so the work is complete (b), rather than that the writer simply stopped writing upon reaching the required number of words (c).

110. D: Having classmates offer peer reviews (a), having the teacher evaluate their work (b), and comparing their work to that of their classmates (c) are all valuable sources of feedback for students about their performance and progress in speaking and enacting through oral reports and presentations as they give different perspectives; however, video recordings of student performance (d) are the only type of completely objective feedback among these choices because they provide an exact record of what the student did. This enables students to self-monitor, make changes/improvements, and appreciate their own progress over time.

Practice Test #2

1. Of the following books, which was published during the Romantic period of literature?
   a. *Leaves of Grass* by Walt Whitman
   b. *Sense and Sensibility* by Jane Austen
   c. *On the Origin of Species* by Charles Darwin
   d. *Far from the Madding Crowd* by Thomas Hardy

2. Before Charles Darwin published *On the Origin of Species,* which of the following reflected resistance to ideas of evolution like his, based on historical context?
   a. Georges Buffon's earlier suggestions concerning potentially common ancestries of similar species
   b. Georges Cuvier's established proof of extinction from comparing fossils and contemporary bones
   c. Carl Linnaeus's classification and John Ray's taxonomy viewing species as divinely designed and unchanging
   d. Jean-Baptiste Lamarck's theory of environmental adaptation, heredity, and increasing complexity

3. In a play, when an actor says something that informs the audience while other characters appear not to hear it, what is the correct terminology for this?
   a. Aside
   b. Soliloquy
   c. Dialogue
   d. Monologue

4. Of the following sentences, which one uses metaphors to create figurative meanings?
   a. He became a tiger in the boxing ring, but he turned into a pussycat at dinner afterward.
   b. He was like a tiger in the boxing ring, but later during dinner, he was just like a pussycat.
   c. He fought so fiercely in the boxing ring, but afterward at dinner he was gentle and kind.
   d. He was ferocious when he was boxing, but he was sweet and gentle in social situations.

5. Which of these is a term that is NOT typically used about a literary dramatic work?
   a. Act
   b. Scene
   c. Stanza
   d. Chapter

6. "A Dialogue of Self and Soul" by William Butler Yeats belongs to which literary genre/subgenre?
   a. Essay
   b. Drama
   c. Poetry
   d. Fiction

Copyright © Mometrix Media. You have been licensed one copy of this document for personal use only. Any other reproduction or redistribution is strictly prohibited. All rights reserved.

7. In which of the following literary forms is the element of literary devices such as similes, metaphors, personification, etc. *most* prominent?

    a. Plays
    b. Poems
    c. Nonfiction
    d. Short stories

8. Which of these literary masterpieces is NOT an epic poem?

    a. Dante's *Divine Comedy*
    b. Milton's *Paradise Lost*
    c. James Joyce's *Ulysses*
    d. Spenser's *The Faerie Queene*

9. Among the following, which element is found exclusively in only one genre of literature?

    a. Plot
    b. Characters
    c. Stage directions
    d. Rhymed/free verse

10. What is true regarding a fundamental contrast between fiction and drama as literary genres? Select ALL correct answers.

    a. Aristotle first defined this contrast between genres.
    b. Plato first articulated this contrast between genres.
    c. Plato first defined it, and Aristotle then developed it.
    d. Fiction did not exist during Plato and Aristotle's day.
    e. What applied to epic then also applies to fiction now.

11. When contrasting the ballad and the sonnet as subgenres of poetry, which of these is accurate?

    a. The ballad is more complex.
    b. The sonnet is more structured.
    c. The ballad is more lyrical.
    d. The sonnet is more narrative.

12. Within the literary genre of poetry, which function is more characteristic of the ballad than the sonnet?

    a. Relating a story about human interactions
    b. Demonstrating skill with writing the poem
    c. Being included as part of theatrical plays
    d. Satirizing romantic, political, and social issues

13. Which of the following characteristics can the fiction subgenres of historical fiction and science fiction be said to share in common?

    a. Both are always about fictional characters.
    b. Both are always about imaginary events.
    c. Both are always speculative in some way.
    d. Both are always closely aligned with facts.

14. According to the ancient Classical definitions, also used by Shakespeare and other playwrights, which of these is NOT necessarily true of the drama subgenres of comedy and tragedy?

  a. Comedy is humorous, and it makes audiences laugh.
  b. Comedy may not be funny, but it has a happy ending.
  c. Tragedy ends in sadness, and it often involves death.
  d. Tragedy inspires terror and pity from the audience.

15. Which of the following is an example of a case when second-person narrative voice or point of view might be more effective than first- or third- person?

  a. An informative text explaining how to install a piece of equipment correctly
  b. A fictional text recounting a dream the narrator had the night before
  c. A persuasive essay concerning a political viewpoint
  d. A petition written by a group of people desiring change

16. To respond to all students' individual and group identities and needs in inclusive educational programs, what must teachers do?

  a. Teachers must meet student needs rather than parent/family needs.
  b. Teachers must meet student needs but not express their own needs.
  c. Teachers must meet their own needs through team problem-solving.
  d. Teachers must meet their own needs through independent solutions.

17. Among the following major types of conflicts typically included in literary plots, which one is classified as an internal conflict?

  a. Man against man
  b. Man against nature
  c. Man against society
  d. Man against himself

18. Which of these is most accurate about functions dialogue can serve in fictional literature?

  a. Dialogue can serve plot advancement but not character development.
  b. Dialogue can serve to illuminate themes and meanings and redirect plots.
  c. Dialogue can serve to set character tone and voice more than motives.
  d. Dialogue can serve to reproduce real speech instead of adding drama.

19. What is true about some ways a reader can analyze character development in literary texts?

  a. Observing differences in what the author vs. other characters say about a character can help.
  b. Observing contradictions in a character's thoughts, words, and deeds cannot inform anything.
  c. Observing the ways in which the author describes each character informs style, nothing else.
  d. Observing the kinds of observations the author makes regarding each character is irrelevant.

20. Of the following statements, which correctly describes research findings about effective writing instruction techniques?
- a. Exposing students to the processes of writing is sufficient.
- b. Teacher modeling and think-alouds are deemed effective.
- c. Providing students with scaffolding is an unneeded crutch.
- d. Implicit and embedded instruction is better than explicit instruction.

21. Among these procedural devices that help students plan and revise writing, which one is for helping them remember key sets of information?
- a. Mnemonic devices
- b. Graphic organizers
- c. Making outlines
- d. Using checklists

22. In literary plot structure, what is correct about the differences between story and discourse?
- a. Discourse is what is produced from the authors' imaginations.
- b. Story is comprised of the words written down by the authors.
- c. Discourse is settings, characters, and events; story arranges them.
- d. Story is what authors invent, while discourse is a story's organization.

23. When composing dialogue in literary fiction, which of these should writers do?
- a. Slow down the story or plot movement through dialogue.
- b. Express their own opinions through character dialogue.
- c. Include only dialogue serving the purposes of the story.
- d. Insert similes or metaphors that show their cleverness.

24. The first sentence of *The Bell Jar* by Sylvia Plath is as follows: "It was a queer, sultry summer, the summer they electrocuted the Rosenbergs, and I didn't know what I was doing in New York." What is most accurate about this sentence?
- a. It establishes setting and character elements via literal meaning.
- b. It establishes the symbols to be used throughout in an allegory.
- c. It establishes the setting for a historical novel about the 1950s.
- d. It establishes an extended metaphor using figurative meaning.

Answer the next two questions based on the excerpt below:

> African-American youth are more likely to miss school because they face more barriers to attendance, such as logistical challenges (such as unreliable transportation), school suspension/expulsion or residential instability (consider homelessness or frequent moves). Fortunately, there is an old proverb that guides us to the solution: it takes a village to ensure that all children, especially African-American children, are present in order to learn and develop on a consistent basis.
>
> (Lauren Mims, Fellow, White House Initiative on Educational Excellence, HOMEROOM – official US Department of Education [ED] blog, 10/07/2015)

25. How does this author provide textual evidence of the barriers to attendance she mentions?
   a. She does not provide any evidence of them.
   b. She provides it with parenthetical examples.
   c. She provides it by alluding to an old proverb.
   d. She provides it only by implicit assumptions.

26. Of which barriers to attendance for African-American students does the author offer examples here?
   a. Logistical challenges
   b. Suspension/expulsion
   c. Residential instability
   d. (a) and (c) but not (b)

27. Which element of Herman Melville's novel *Moby-Dick* reflects how he develops the basic, even universal, theme of fate?
   a. Ishmael's multidisciplinary pursuit for whale knowledge
   b. Ahab's attempts to interpret the character of Moby-Dick
   c. Ahab's convincing sailors that his quest is their shared destiny
   d. White sailors' standing/walking upon black slaves/sailors

Answer the next three questions based on the excerpt below.

Mamzelle Aurélie possessed a good strong figure, ruddy cheeks, hair that was changing from brown to gray, and a determined eye. She wore a man's hat about the farm and an old blue army overcoat when it was cold, and sometimes top boots.
Mamzelle Aurélie had never thought of marrying. She had never been in love. At the age of 20 she had received a proposal, which she had promptly declined, and at the age of 50, she had not yet lived to regret it.
So she was quite alone in the world, except for her dog Ponto, and the negroes who lived in her cabins and worked her crops, and the fowls, a few cows, a couple of mules, her gun (with which she shot chicken-hawks), and her religion.
     ("Regret" by Kate Chopin)

28. Which type of characterization does the author give in the first paragraph?
   a. She makes direct characterization.
   b. She uses indirect characterization.
   c. Direct and indirect characterization
   d. No characterization, just description

29. In the second paragraph, what method of characterization does the author use?
   a. Direct
   b. Indirect
   c. Neither
   d. Both

30. This passage's third paragraph consists of which of these?
  a. A description without any added characterization
  b. Direct characterization throughout that sentence
  c. Mostly description, some indirect characterization
  d. Direct and indirect characterization in equal parts

Answer the next five questions based on the following stanzas from Alfred, Lord Tennyson's "The Charge of the Light Brigade"

Half a league, half a league, 1

Half a league onward, 2

All in the valley of Death 3

Rode the six hundred. 4

"Forward, the Light Brigade! 5

Charge for the guns!" he said. 6

Into the valley of Death 7

Rode the six hundred. 8

"Forward, the Light Brigade!" 9

Was there a man dismayed? 10

Not though the soldier knew 11

Someone had blundered. 12

Theirs not to make reply, 13

Theirs not to reason why, 14

Theirs but to do and die. 15

Into the valley of Death 16

Rode the six hundred. 17

31. What is the *first* literary device with which Tennyson opens the first stanza above?
  a. Metaphor
  b. Repetition
  c. Hyperbole
  d. Imagery

32. What effect(s) does the poet accomplish with the sound of the first two lines?
  a. Creates a marching rhythm
  b. Makes the distance seem less
  c. Establishes a weary mood
  d. (a) and (c) rather than (b)

33. What is reflected by the word choice of "the valley of Death?"
a. Allusion to a Biblical psalm
b. The use of a metaphor
c. (a) and (b), but not (d)
d. The use of a simile

34. What are the primary meter and rhyme scheme of the first stanza?
a. Dactylic dimeter, AABCDDDEC
b. Iambic pentameter, ABACDCDED
c. Trochaic tetrameter, AABBCDCDE
d. Anapestic heptameter, ABACBDDCE

35. How do the form and word choice of lines 13–15 in the second stanza contribute to their meaning?
a. They reflect the complexity of the battle by using plenty of variety.
b. They reflect the men's heroic humility and honesty using simplicity.
c. They reflect the treacherous nature of war by the use of irregularity.
d. They reflect the tedium of the soldier's life through their monotony.

36. A type of figurative language that uses description to access the reader's senses is known as...
a. Simile
b. Imagery
c. Metaphor
d. Hyperbole

37. Of the following, which word is NOT an example of the figurative quality of onomatopoeia?
a. Hum
b. Click
c. Buzz
d. Dog

38. Regarding the reading strategy of summarizing text, which of the following is most accurate about what will help students support their reading comprehension?
a. It will help them to identify important ideas, but not to organize them.
b. It will help them to identify themes, problems, and solutions in a text.
c. It will help them to monitor comprehension more than to sequence it.
d. It will help them to make visual the connections with text they realize.

39. When evaluating the strength of a prediction on the basis of textual evidence, which of these identifies the best literary analysis supported by the best textual evidence?
a. The analysis shows special insight supported by strong, relevant, and accurate evidence.
b. The analysis shows reasonable understanding with relevant, clear, and accurate evidence.
c. The analysis shows reasonable understanding and generalized and/or partial evidence.
d. The analysis shows generalized understanding, including pertinent and accurate evidence.

40. Two groups of students are assigned to compare texts. One group is given speeches by Abraham Lincoln and Stephen Douglas about slavery. The other group is given essays by an author from the Enlightenment and one from the Romantic movement about nature. What are the students most likely to conclude?

    a. Both groups will find that both texts conflict.
    b. One pair of texts will conflict; one will agree.
    c. Both groups will find both texts to be similar.
    d. One pair of texts differs greatly; one differs slightly.

41. Which of these is an example of using a metaphor in informational text?

    a. Writing that a racehorse ran like the wind
    b. Writing of the cloud of the Great Depression
    c. Writing that a racehorse ran unbelievably fast
    d. Writing of the gloom caused by the Depression

42. Of the following, which expression that could be found in informational text uses words in a literal sense rather than a figurative one? Select all choices that apply.

    a. An onslaught of criticism
    b. An avalanche of rumors
    c. A throng of onlookers
    d. A gaggle of women
    e. A belligerent mob

43. When reading informational text, what is applicable about inferences that readers draw?

    a. Drawing inferences helps readers to fill in information not stated in the text.
    b. Drawing inferences helps readers answer questions, not understand a text.
    c. Drawing inferences requires knowing text information, not prior knowledge.
    d. Drawing inferences produces subjective rather than objective interpretation.

44. If someone is reading a nonfiction biography/autobiography, which of these is NOT one of the most suitable inferences that a reader might draw about the text?

    a. About actions that the subject of the text takes
    b. About the events that are described in the text
    c. About problems and solutions the text presents
    d. About what message the author communicates

45. Which of these must students be able to do in order to understand, critically judge, draw conclusions about, and individually interpret informational text that they read?

    a. Locate instead of organize evidence in a text
    b. Organize information without differentiating
    c. Differentiate main ideas from details in a text
    d. Infer about text without any prior knowledge

46. In analyzing how the author of a biology text connects and distinguishes among concepts, a teacher helps students identify animals categorized by diet as carnivores, herbivores, or omnivores. Which exercise(s) will help students most to identify author comparison and contrast of categories?

   a. Assigning sentence frames
   b. Assigning cloze procedures
   c. Assigning memorizing terms
   d. (a) and (b) will help more than (c)

47. How can teachers use portfolio assessments to evaluate student writing?

   a. As formative assessments
   b. As summative assessments
   c. As both kinds of assessments
   d. As neither kind of assessment

48. A politician supports a point by quoting a statement made by member of the same party. The politician's opponent from the other party refutes the quotation, saying, "Consider the source!" This is an example of using rhetoric to support one's position through which persuasive technique often used in the media?

   a. Ad hominem
   b. Majority belief
   c. Scapegoating
   d. Using denial

49. Which word is a definite article?

   a. A
   b. An
   c. The
   d. None is.

50. "She likes hiking, swimming, rowing, and to climb mountains." Which type of error does this sentence demonstrate?

   a. A run-on sentence
   b. A dangling participle
   c. A sentence fragment
   d. A lack of parallelism

51. Which of the following is mechanically correct?

   a. I saw that the machine did not work because there was a problem with it's motor.
   b. I seen that the machine did not work because there was a problem with its motor.
   c. I saw that the machine did not work because there was a problem with its motor.
   d. I seen that the machine did not work because there was a problem with it's motor.

52. The text feature of boldface is most often used to indicate which of these?

   a. A word that has a footnote at the page bottom
   b. A word that is listed and defined in the glossary
   c. The words of the captions accompanying visuals
   d. The words of all text in sidebars on some pages

53. Which of these is a correct statement about how to use a rubric relative to writing instruction and/or assessment?
   a. Students should use a rubric as a guide in what and how to write.
   b. The teacher should not explain the rubric to students in advance.
   c. Rubrics are for teachers to use in assessment and not otherwise.
   d. Teachers should only use rubrics for organizing their lesson plans.

54. To teach students how to differentiate between denotations and connotations of words in informational texts, what is the best instructional strategy?
   a. Sample sentences with multiple-choice meanings
   b. Sample sentences using each for the same words
   c. Sample sentences that do either or both of these
   d. Sample sentences which do neither one of these

55. Among the following hypothetical sentences for a scientific text (e.g., a research journal article), which is/are (an) example(s) of appropriate usage with technical language?
   a. "We identified this as a central component of protein metabolism."
   b. "This was identified as a central component of protein metabolism."
   c. "Fewer than ten reproducible assays make our findings insignificant."
   d. "From our findings we conclude everyone needs these supplements."
   e. "We conclude that more research is needed to isolate this mechanism."

56. In these professors' descriptions of how some students reacted to administering an assessment in a practicum situation, which would represent implicit rather than explicit meaning in an informational text?
   a. "The students, their faces ashen, said, 'We didn't finish giving the test.'"
   b. "The students panicked just because they didn't finish giving the test."
   c. "The students were unable to finish giving the test in the time allotted."
   d. "The students so dreaded breaking protocol that their faces had paled."

57. When a middle school student needs to determine whether written sentences in a worksheet are complete and correct for an assignment, which paper or digital reference material should s/he consult?
   a. A paper or a digital encyclopedia
   b. A physical or an online dictionary
   c. A paper or digital grammar guide
   d. A word-processor grammar check

58. Which of the following will help readers analyze informational text to identify author point of view or purpose when the author does not state this explicitly?
   a. Consider how the author's word choices affect the readers' perceptions of the subject.
   b. Disregard what the author wants to persuade readers of and focus on hidden agendas.
   c. Consider how strong author choices of examples and facts are, not their effects on readers.
   d. Disregard what the author wants to accomplish by writing because only the author knows.

59. "Courage, determination, and perseverance is required for success in this effort." What is grammatically incorrect in this sentence?

  a. There is nothing wrong
  b. Subject-verb agreement
  c. Agreement of verb tense
  d. Lack of parallel structure

60. "He was an old man who fished alone in a skiff in the Gulf Stream and he had gone eighty-four days now without taking a fish." (Ernest Hemingway, *The Old Man and the Sea*, 1953) What type of sentence is this?

  a. A simple sentence
  b. Complex sentence
  c. Compound sentence
  d. Compound–complex

61. What type of sentence includes both independent and dependent clauses?

  a. Complex
  b. Compound
  c. Compound–complex
  d. (a) and (c) but not (b)

62. Which of these versions of the sentence has a compound–complex structure?

  a. She was sick, and so she was not able to attend the party.
  b. She was not able to attend the party because she was sick.
  c. She was feeling sick and was not able to attend the party.
  d. She didn't attend because she was sick; she missed the party.

63. Of the following variations, which one is a simple sentence?

  a. "You could run, but could not hide."
  b. "Although you can run, you can't hide."
  c. "You can run, but you cannot hide."
  d. "Run; run fast, because you can't hide."

64. "He could not finish the test in time even though he tried his hardest." This sentence is of which type?

  a. Compound–complex
  b. Compound
  c. Complex
  d. Simple

65. Linguist Noam Chomsky famously composed the following sentence to prove a point: "Colorless green ideas sleep furiously." What element of language use renders this sentence meaningless?

  a. Incorrect sentence syntax
  b. Contradictory word choice
  c. Lack of proper punctuation
  d. Subject-verb disagreement

66. "To better serve you, we ask that you answer this short survey, it will take less than five minutes." Which common grammatical/mechanical error(s) does this sentence include? Select ALL correct answers.
   a. Inconsistent verb tense
   b. A split infinitive
   c. A comma splice
   d. A misplaced modifier
   e. There are no errors

67. Among seven steps a reader can take to evaluate an author's argument in persuasive writing, which of the first four steps should the reader take *first*?
   a. Evaluate the author's objectivity regarding the issue.
   b. Judge how relevant the supporting evidence provided is.
   c. Identify the author's assumptions regarding the issue.
   d. Identify what supporting evidence the author offers.

68. When authors use rhetoric to support their points of view and/or purposes in informational text, by which of these means can they best provide supporting evidence?
   a. By relating some personal anecdotes
   b. By reporting about some case studies
   c. By making analogies about some ideas
   d. By convincing wording for right and wrong

69. The phrases "jumbo shrimp" or "deafening silence" are examples of which rhetorical device?
   a. Hyperbole
   b. Hyperbaton
   c. Oxymoron
   d. Chiasmus

70. Among author methods of appeal, which of these most persuade readers by making disagreement impossible, so authors can then make them appear to support their positions?
   a. Generalizations
   b. Rhetorical questions
   c. Transfer and association
   d. Humor ridiculing opponents

71. If students in middle school grades are assigned to write text for students in early elementary grades to read, which of the following should they do?
   a. Use script handwriting rather than printing to set examples for the readers.
   b. Use vocabulary, sentence structure, and handwriting on the readers' levels.
   c. Use longer, more complex sentences to provide a challenge for the readers.
   d. Use their usual vocabulary, sentence structure, and handwriting as is natural.

72. When is it most appropriate for students to write in casual language at their own age level?
   a. To share a certain experience with their readers
   b. To get parental permission for a desired activity
   c. To write something for their classmates to read
   d. To write a story that younger children can read

73. Which of the following is accurate regarding paragraph focus and development?
   a. Paragraphs with unrelated sentences are not well developed.
   b. Paragraphs with generalizations but no details are unfocused.
   c. Paragraphs without term definitions or contexts will lack focus.
   d. Paragraphs without needed background are underdeveloped.

74. What structural pattern in a paragraph serves to show readers instead of telling them?
   a. Narration
   b. Description
   c. Classification
   d. Giving examples

75. Which of these is accurate about what readers should do to facilitate critically evaluating the effectiveness of methods of appeal used by informational text authors?
   a. Readers should not waste their time trying to paraphrase the text.
   b. Readers should research all unfamiliar subjects and/or vocabulary.
   c. Readers should consider only effects, not which appeals are used.
   d. Readers should evaluate from an author's presumed perspective.

76. Related to the reader's process of identifying author purposes in writing informational text, which of these is correct?
   a. Stated purposes contradicting other text portions may signal hidden author agendas.
   b. Authors of informational text always state the most important purposes of the text.
   c. The main or central idea of a text means the same thing as the purpose of that text.
   d. Identifying unstated author purposes for texts offers no advantages to the readers.

77. The part of speech that most often forms the predicate of a sentence is which of these?
   a. Verb
   b. Noun
   c. Adjective
   d. Adverb

78. "She completed the challenging task quickly but carefully." In this sentence, what is an adverb?
   a. quickly
   b. (a) and (c)
   c. carefully
   d. challenging

79. Of the following components of a reference citation, which one is needed only for citing electronic sources rather than for both printed and electronic sources?

    a.   Author name
    b.   Publication date
    c.   Book/article title
    d.   The date of access

80. Which of the following major style manuals is _most_ commonly used for research papers on English literature?

    a.   APA style manual
    b.   MLA style manual
    c.   Chicago style manual
    d.   Turabian style manual

81. When incorporating outside sources into a research paper, which of these should students do?

    a.   End papers with quotations
    b.   Include more brief quotations
    c.   Include many longer quotations
    d.   Quote only supporting information

82. For making speeches, which nonverbal behaviors enhance audience perceptions of speaker credibility?

    a.   Making eye contact with certain listeners
    b.   Making random/unrelated body motions
    c.   Making startling/novel facial expressions
    d.   Making gestures congruent with meaning

83. Of the following attributes of mobile and text media for presenting ideas in public communications, which is a disadvantage?

    a.   Popularity
    b.   Timeliness
    c.   Interactivity
    d.   Limited length

84. When comparing digital media to print media, which is/are the greatest digital advantage(s)?

    a.   Permanence
    b.   (c) and (d)
    c.   Versatility
    d.   Flexibility

85. An advertisement for a prescription eye drop features a woman identified as a doctor, who both recommends the product to a patient, and she also says she uses it herself with good results. This involves which method(s) of appeal?

    a.   Expert opinion
    b.   Testimonial
    c.   Bandwagon
    d.   (a) and (b)

86. Which of the following is an example of a bandwagon method of appeal?

    a. A car is advertised with a beautiful model sitting in it.
    b. A soap ad shows someone bathing under a waterfall.
    c. An ad sings, "Wouldn't you like to be a pepper, too?"
    d. A brand made in USA is shown with an American flag.

87. Among the elements of a written argument, which one do statistics and examples most represent?

    a. Claims
    b. Reasons
    c. Evidence
    d. Counterclaims

88. MATCHING: To assess the soundness of author reasoning, logical fallacies should be identified and negated. Place the number of the Latin term for each logical fallacy in the space next to the letter choice with the statement corresponding to it.

    a. "All great societies have always done it this way." ___ 1. *Argumentum ad verecundiam*
    b. "This is true: nobody has ever proven it was false." ___ 2. *Argumentum ad populum*
    c. "Drugs are bad, drugs are bad, drugs are bad," etc. ___ 3. *Argumentum ad ignorantiam*
    d. "He's a brilliant scientist, so his politics are valid." ___ 4. *Argumentum ad nauseam*

89. Suppose a written or spoken argument's claim is that community colleges in your state have recently had their budgets cut. Which of these would be sufficient evidence to prove this claim?

    a. Citing the largest budget cut at one college
    b. Citing two prominent examples of the cuts
    c. Citing examples from 15 of 34 state colleges
    d. Citing specific cut amounts at all 34 colleges

90. "Going to the beach for the day, an enjoyable pastime." This is an example of what grammatical error?

    a. There is no error in the sentence.
    b. Subject-verb agreement
    c. Lack of parallel structure
    d. It is a sentence fragment

91. According to research findings, which of these is an example of effective instructional practices to support English language acquisition for ELL students?

    a. Encouraging independence by assigning projects only individually
    b. Writing problems and directions in shorter and simpler sentences
    c. Emphasizing how quickly students finish work, not how accurately
    d. Asking only questions they can answer using lower level cognition

92. The Cognitive Academic Language Learning Approach (CALLA) is found to be helpful for middle school ELL students. What is true of this approach?

    a. It includes content objectives but does not include language objectives.
    b. It includes language objectives but does not include content objectives.
    c. It has content and language objectives, but there are none for learning strategies.
    d. It allows thematically based content or formats using sheltered content.

93. When establishing ground rules for collaborative student discussions, which of these should teachers include?

    a. Teachers should encourage students by allowing them to jump in with comments at any time.

    b. Teachers should encourage talkative students to hold forth to take pressure off of shyer ones.

    c. Teachers should include in student discussions ground rules that students must not engage in cross talk.

    d. Teachers should include rules against verbal abuse, but physical abuse is too unlikely for rules.

94. Which of the following sentence versions is mechanically correct?

    a. You're nametag is in it's place on the table.

    b. Your nametag is in it's place on the table.

    c. You're nametag is in its place on the table.

    d. Your nametag is in its place on the table.

95. Which of the following is a phrase rather than a clause?

    a. He died.

    b. It's raining.

    c. A very good time.

    d. Then we went out.

96. A middle school ELA teacher wants to avoid assigning traditional homework wherein students must research a topic and report their findings to the class. Instead, she wants to enable students to make more positive connections by responding to stimuli in a web-based tool as homework, which will also stimulate classroom discussion more effectively. Which technology tool would accomplish this best?

    a. Blog

    b. Podcast

    c. RSS feed

    d. Videoconference

97. Based on vocabulary words you can think of beginning with *trans-*, what does this prefix mean?

    a. Across

    b. Change

    c. Carrying

    d. Different

98. Which of the following research-based strategies or approaches for writing instruction is characterized by setting clear writing goals, observing concrete data, and applying learning to written composition?

    a. Prewriting strategies

    b. Modeling strategies

    c. Inquiry strategies

    d. Process writing

99. Which common mode of writing is most characterized by the author's assumption that certain things are facts or truths?

    a. Informative
    b. Descriptive
    c. Persuasive
    d. Narrative

100. In evaluating reading strategies, the US Department of Education's What Works Clearinghouse has reported strong and moderate research evidence for five recommendations of effective practices in teaching adolescent reading. Of these, which ones have strong evidence? Select ALL correct answers.

    a. Instructing students explicitly for learning vocabulary
    b. Explicit, direct instruction in comprehension strategies
    c. Enhancing student interest and involvement in reading
    d. Intensive specialist interventions for struggling readers
    e. Enabling students to discuss text meaning/interpretation

101. According to the Center on Instruction (COI), which of the choices below accurately describes one of several recommendations for teaching adolescent literacy?

    a. Teach effective use of comprehension strategies only in discrete lessons.
    b. Set high standards for text and vocabulary, not questions or conversation.
    c. Focus on student engagement during reading more than motivation to read.
    d. Instruct necessary content knowledge for students' crucial concept mastery.

102. Among the following, which is NOT a common purpose for writing in a journal?

    a. Documenting experiences with terminal illness
    b. Chronicling experiences with addiction recovery
    c. Travel to or life in other countries and spiritual journeys
    d. Relating the story of a fictional plot and characters

103. When evaluating writing strategies, what does research find about effective instruction of middle school students?

    a. Explicit instruction is best for teaching specific tasks, such as writing argumentative essays.
    b. Explicit instruction is better for teaching brainstorming, editing, or other general processes.
    c. Explicit instruction is necessary to teach specific, general, planning, and compositional tasks.
    d. Explicit instruction is more important to teach revising and editing than planning for writing.

104. If a teacher assigns students to pairs for cooperative writing partnerships, which of the following should their activities include?

    a. One student should write, and the other should review the work.
    b. Each partner in a pair takes turns being the writer and the reviewer.
    c. Each student should provide only positive feedback to the other.
    d. Each student should give only constructive feedback to another.

105. Which of the following reflects a sound principle for writing blog posts?
a. Punctuation is less important online than in print.
b. Paragraphs should be the same length as in print.
c. All blank spaces should be eliminated in any blog.
d. A post should have a beginning, middle, and end.

106. Which of these is more characteristic of a summative assessment?
a. The teacher administers it frequently during instruction.
b. The teacher uses its results to inform teaching changes.
c. The teacher gives it after lessons, units, or school years are complete.
d. The teacher relies on it for individualizing student data.

107. Among assessments, which of these is typical of formative ones?
a. They are most often criterion-referenced tests.
b. They are most frequently norm-referenced tests.
c. They are most frequently standardized measures.
d. They are most often the most objective measures.

108. What approach would be most appropriate for teachers to solicit reflective responses from students about how their ELA curriculum and assessments are designed and used?
a. Having students take questionnaires
b. Having students write in journals
c. Having students rate teachers
d. Having students write essays

109. A teacher plans to use a rubric to define learning objectives for a class instructional unit, guide students in completing their assignments, and serve as a unit assessment. Which statement is most applicable to incorporating student input into assessment design?
a. So many premade rubrics are available online, it is unnecessary to "reinvent the wheel."
b. Only the teacher, who knows learning objectives and how to do it, should create a rubric.
c. The teacher should collect student input on objectives and assignments to create a rubric.
d. The students and teacher should all work together in designing the rubric collaboratively.

110. Of the following, which most accurately reflects how students can use the most appropriate kinds of writing according to their purposes?
a. Students who want to get readers to agree with them use argumentative writing.
b. Students who want to tell a story and the lesson it affords use speculative writing.
c. Students who want to invite readers to explore ideas must use descriptive writing.
d. Students who want to share an experience with readers can use narrative writing.

Constructed Response

1. <u>Textual Interpretation:</u> Based on the following excerpt, write a response that answers the questions following it.

> Most terribly cold it was; it snowed, and was nearly quite dark, and evening-- the last evening of the year. In this cold and darkness there went along the street a poor little girl, bareheaded, and with naked feet. When she left home she had slippers on, it is true; but what was the good of that? They were very large slippers, which her mother had hitherto worn; so large were they; and the poor little thing lost them as she scuffled away across the street, because of two carriages that rolled by dreadfully fast.
>
> One slipper was nowhere to be found; the other had been laid hold of by an urchin, and off he ran with it; he thought it would do capitally for a cradle when he some day or other should have children himself. So the little maiden walked on with her tiny naked feet, that were quite red and blue from cold. She carried a quantity of matches in an old apron, and she held a bundle of them in her hand. Nobody had bought anything of her the whole livelong day; no one had given her a single farthing.
>
> She crept along trembling with cold and hunger--a very picture of sorrow, the poor little thing!
>
> (From "The Little Match Girl" by Hans Christian Andersen)

What is the narrative point of view of the author?

Give specific examples from this text of how Andersen establishes setting, character, and situation.

What kind of mood does these opening paragraphs establish? How does the author create this mood?

2. <u>Teaching Writing:</u> A sixth-grade class had an assignment to write a descriptive essay about a memorable experience during their summer vacation, with their classmates as the audience. The following is an example of one student's essay. Read the essay and then write a response that completes the numbered items following the essay example.

> I have to say the highlight of my summer vacation was our family's trip to Europe. I have never been to any other country before. On this trip we went to several countries. We saw, heard, felt, smelled, and tasted lots of new things.
>
> First we went to Spain. I got to see the Alhambra in Granada and the Prado Museum and Royal Palace in Madrid.
>
> Then we went to France. In Paris I got to see the Eiffel Tower, the Arc de Triomphe, and the Louvre. We also went to the French countryside. It was beautiful.
>
> Then we went to Italy. I got to see the canals in Venice, the Roman Colosseum, the Leaning Tower of Pisa, and the Vatican in Vatican City in Rome.
>
> Then we went to Germany. I got to see the Brandenburg Gate in Berlin, the Cologne Cathedral in Cologne, and the Heidelberg Castle in Heidelberg.
>
> I heard different languages in every country. Some people spoke English, but a lot of people did not. Every country had different kinds of food. They also had different kinds of music. They had different customs in different countries. I liked this trip to Europe because so many things there were new and different to me.

1. Identify one strength in this student's writing. Provide several examples of this strength from the text that support your identification. Do NOT include grammar, punctuation, or other writing conventions.

2. Identify one weakness in this student's writing. Provide several examples of this weakness from the text that support your identification. Do NOT include grammar, punctuation, or other writing conventions.

3. Give a description of one follow-up assignment you could give the student of this essay which would either expand upon the strength you identified in #1, OR would remediate the weakness you identified in #2. Explain how this assignment would help the student improve his or her writing.

Answer Key and Explanations

1. B: Jane Austen's novel (1811) was written during the Romantic period of English literature (1798-1832). Walt Whitman's (1855) book of poetry (a), Charles Darwin's (1859) nonfiction scientific work (c), and Thomas Hardy's (1874) novel (d) were all written during the Victorian period of English literature (1832-1870).

2. C: Before Charles Darwin published *On the Origin of Species* (1859), Georges Buffon suggested (1766) some similar-looking animal species could share common ancestries, supporting ideas of evolution (a). Georges Cuvier's paleontology research found fossils of past species resembling modern animal versions (1799), proving extinction (b) and supporting functional adaptation. Jean-Baptiste Lamarck's (1809) theory that life forms adapted to environments, inherited adaptations, and developed increasing complexity (d) supported Darwin's ideas. Carl Linnaeus (1735) and John Ray's (1686-1691) work showed resistance to ideas of evolution, reflecting the Royal Society's post-English Civil War (1642-1651) reaction—both against science threatening stability, and for science maintaining it.

3. A: When an actor in a play says something to inform the audience which the other characters do not hear, this is called an aside. A soliloquy (b) is when an actor speaks a longer piece of dialogue alone. A monologue (c) is a synonym for a soliloquy. A dialogue (d) is a conversation between or among two or more characters; the term dialogue (without the article) also refers to speech within plays overall, but a speech by a single character is never called *a* dialogue.

4. A: This sentence uses two metaphors (implied comparisons): "He became a tiger" and "he turned into a pussycat." These give readers more understanding of the subject "he" by comparing his qualities, characteristics, and/or behaviors to those of more familiar examples—in this case, to contrasting salient qualities of two different members of the same felid family. Sentence (b) also makes this comparison using figurative language, but with similes (explicit comparisons) instead of metaphors. Sentences (c) and (d) both use literal meanings rather than figurative ones.

5. D: Literary dramatic works, i.e., comedies, tragedies, and other plays, are divided into major sections called acts (a) (even one-act plays have an "act"), and each act is subdivided into scenes (b). Each scene typically is defined by being in a different place and/or time and/or by involving different characters and/or action. Shakespeare and many other playwrights (e.g., ancient Greek, Medieval, Renaissance, Elizabethan, etc.) composed their dramas in poetic verse, so these include stanzas (c), the poetic version of paragraphs. Chapters (d) are divisions not of dramas but of fictional and nonfictional books.

6. C: "A Dialogue of Self and Soul" is a poem. Yeats also wrote a number of masterful essays and a nonfiction book (*A Vision*), but he is most known and lauded for his poetry. This piece is not an essay (a), a subgenre of nonfiction. Despite the word "dialogue" in the title, it is neither a drama (b) nor a novel or other work of fiction (d).

7. B: Poems are the literary forms that most prominently use literary devices such as similes, metaphors, personification, etc. Although authors of plays (a); nonfiction (c) essays, books, etc.; and fictional short stories (d) may certainly use such devices (to varying extents depending on author purpose and style), those literary devices named are most prominently found in poems.

8. C: Dante Alighieri's *Divine Comedy* (*Inferno*, *Purgatorio*, and *Paradiso*) (a) is an epic poem and a religious allegory. John Milton's *Paradise Lost* (b) is also an epic poem and religious allegory, and so

57

is Edmund Spenser's *The Faerie Queene* (d). However, James Joyce's *Ulysses* (c) is a novel, not a poem. Though Joyce wanted this novel to be an epic, modeled its chapters on adventures of Ulysses (Odysseus) in Homer's epic poem the *Odyssey,* and drew parallels between his characters and Homer's, this book is nevertheless a Modernist novel with elements of realism rather than an epic poem.

9. C: Only the genre of drama includes stage directions, which tell actors where, how, and what they should do physically in plays, which are written to be performed. Plots (a) are found in plays, novels, short stories, and even some poems. Characters (b) are also found in all of these genres. And many plays, particularly early (e.g., ancient Greek; Shakespeare's and other Elizabethan/Renaissance playwrights' work, etc.) as well as some modern and postmodern ones, are written in rhymed and/or free verse (d).

10. B, C, D, and E: A fundamental contrast between fiction and drama is that drama uses direct imitation, i.e., actors portray characters, whereas fiction combines some direct imitation with exposition and narrative. Actually, the concept of fiction (and of fictional extended prose narrative) did not exist during Plato and Aristotle's time (d); however, they contrasted epic versus drama, and the distinctions they made regarding epic works apply equally to fictional works today (e). Plato first defined this contrast (b), and subsequently Aristotle developed it further (c). Hence only (a) is untrue.

11. B: Ballads are less complex than sonnets, not more (a). Sonnets have developed at least five forms: Petrarchan/Italian, Occitan, Shakespearean/English, Spenserian, and Modern are the major ones, but each has its own specific rhyme scheme; all but the Modern have regular meter, and overall, the sonnet form is more structured (b). Although ballads were popularly called "lyrical ballads" in the eighteenth century when they were often set to music, the ballad is actually narrative (c) because it tells a story, whereas the sonnet is lyrical (d) due to its regular rhyme and meter (*sonnet* derives from the Italian *sonetto,* i.e., "little song").

12. A: One major defining characteristic of the ballad is its narrative function. Traditional ballads tell stories of love, jealousy, revenge, murder, etc.; broadside ballads were composed to entertain and inform the common people about current events; literary ballads enabled intellectuals and the socially elite to express themselves artistically. Historical functions of the sonnet include demonstrating one's skill writing in a highly structured poetic form (b); being featured prominently in theatrical plays (c) (some early plays included ballads, but not to the extent of sonnets); and satirizing romantic, political, and social issues of the time (d).

13. C: Although both subgenres are fiction, they are not always about fictional *characters* (a): some tell fictional *stories* about *real* characters—e.g., Anthony Burgess's novel *Nothing Like the Sun* about what he imagined as Shakespeare's life, or Mary Renault's *The Bull from the Sea* about her conception of Theseus (apparently historical figure and myth combined) and the Minotaur. Similarly, other historical and science fiction may contain only fictional characters' fictional individual experiences, but within actual events—e.g., Esther Forbes' novel *Johnny Tremain*, set before and during the American Revolution. Thomas Pynchon's historical novel *Against the Day*; science fiction novels *Earth* by David Brin, *Callahan's Key* by Spider Robinson, *The Astronauts* by Stanislaw Lem; and many others were based on a 1908 explosion (probably from a meteorite or comet) in Tunguska, Siberia. Numerous other examples exist. Some historical and science fiction works are closely aligned with facts; others are far more imaginative (d). Because they are ultimately fiction, both involve some kind of speculation (c).

14. A: Although the popular modern definition of comedy equates it with humor and making people laugh, this was NOT the ancient Greeks' Classical definition, to which Shakespeare and others also adhered, that comedy may or may not be funny, but it always has a happy ending (b). Ancient Greek, Elizabethan and Renaissance, and modern definitions of tragedy all include sad endings, often involving death (c). According to Aristotle, tragedy should evoke audience emotional responses of terror and pity (d) to be effective.

15. A: Directions for installation are the most likely of the choices to contain the word "you," particularly as the reader of the text should be personally following the instructions given (i.e. "You will next remove the orange cap to access the tank."). (b) and (c) would both be more likely to use the first-person pronoun "I" than the second-person "you". (d) is more likely to contain the third-person pronoun "we."

16. C: In inclusive educational programs, teachers must meet not only student needs, but also the needs of students' parents and families (a); effectively communicate their own needs (b); and be willing to find solutions to their own needs through team-based problem-solving (c) rather than seeking solutions independently (d).

17. D: Among these major types of conflicts found in literary plots, man against man (a), man against nature (b), and man against society (c) are all classified as external conflicts because they involve a struggle between a character and someone or something outside that character. The conflict of man against himself (d) is classified as an internal conflict because it involves an interior struggle within one character.

18. B: Dialogue can not only advance a story and plot, but also support and inform character development (a). It can illuminate themes or meanings in the story and change the direction of a plot (b). It can establish story tone, character tone, narrative voice, and character voice as well as illuminate character motivations and wishes for readers (c). Additionally, dialogue can reproduce real-life speech patterns authentically and even add drama to a story via representing conflicts and the actions that ensue from them (d).

19. A: Some things readers can do to understand literary characters and how authors develop them include observing differences in what the author says about a character vs. what other characters say about him or her (a); observing contradictions in what a character thinks, says, and does (b); observing the ways the author describes each individual character, which informs not only writing style but also how the author develops each character respectively (c); and observing what kinds of observations the author makes about each character, which is very relevant (d) to how the author wants readers to perceive them differently.

20. B: Research into writing instruction has found that exposing students to writing processes is NOT sufficient (a). Additional teaching techniques are needed, including teacher modeling and think-alouds, which have been found effective (b); providing students with temporary support, gradually fading it as their skills grow, i.e., scaffolding (c); and explicit instruction, found more effective than implicit or embedded instruction (d).

21. A: Mnemonic devices help with remembering information by organizing it into patterns, e.g., rebus-like arrangement of initial letters to form acronyms (like remembering the 12 cranial nerves with "On Old Olympus's Towering Top, A Finn And German Viewed A Hop"). Graphic organizers (b) help with making abstract concepts and relationships visual, e.g., Venn diagrams show both similarities and differences. Making outlines (c) helps with identifying and organizing main ideas and supporting details. Checklists (d) help ensure one has completed all steps or components of a task or project, and with self-analysis and/or self-assessment.

22. D: What authors produce from their imaginations is part of the definition of story, not discourse (a). The words that authors write down are part of the definition of discourse, not story (b). Story includes settings, characters, and events whereas discourse arranges those story elements, not vice versa (c). Thus writers invent the story, and the ways in which they then organize it are discourse (d).

23. C: When composing fictional dialogue, writers should NOT let that dialogue slow down the movement of the story or plot (a), use the dialogue for expressing their own opinions (b) instead of those of the characters speaking, or self-consciously insert similes or metaphors to show how clever they are as writers (d); these are unnatural in real conversation and will read awkwardly in written dialogue. However, all dialogue SHOULD serve the story's purpose(s), rather than be irrelevant conversations in quotation marks.

24. A: Plath opens her semiautobiographical novel by establishing the time, place, and main character's feelings of confusion and disaffection through a statement with literal meaning. This book is not an allegory, and the meaning of its first sentence is not symbolic (b). Its nature is closer to a thinly fictionalized memoir than a historical novel (c). The opening sentence quoted does not use figurative meaning, and the novel is not characterized by any overarching extended metaphor (d).

25. B: The author uses examples enclosed in parentheses of the general categories she identifies among barriers to attendance. Both the general categories and parenthetical examples supply textual evidence. Therefore, (a) is incorrect. When she alludes to the old (African) proverb (c), which is "It takes a village to raise a child," she is not providing textual evidence of attendance barriers; her allusion is to support her point about the solution. Since she states categories and examples of barriers explicitly, (d) is also incorrect.

26. D: The author gives an example of logistical challenges (a) as unreliable transportation, and examples of residential instability (c) as homelessness and moving frequently. However, she does not give any examples of suspension or expulsion (b): because being suspended or being expelled is a barrier, examples of these are neither needed nor really possible.

27. C: Melville's development of the basic, even universal, theme of fate—and in this case, how it can be misleading, may not exist, or is ultimately unknowable by humans—is reflected in Ahab's manipulating his crew to believe that his obsessive personal quest for Moby-Dick is also their shared destiny. Ishmael's pursuit for knowledge about whales (a) in an unsuccessful effort to understand Moby-Dick reflects Melville's development of the theme of humankind's finite understanding. Ahab's attempts to interpret Moby-Dick's nature (b) also reflects Melville's development of the same theme, with the whale symbolizing God, whose nature is also humanly unknowable. White sailors' standing/walking on black slaves/sailors (d) reflects Melville's development of the theme of exploitation of indigenous peoples, which whaling shared with unfair trade, buffalo hunting, gold mining, and other elements of white territorial expansionism.

28. B: By describing the character's appearance, the author provides indirect characterization: Her strong figure suggests a strong character; her ruddy cheeks imply vigorous health and personality; her determined eye implies a determined spirit; even her dress suggests an independent woman. Thus, Chopin shows rather than tells readers what Mamzelle Aurélie is like. Telling would be direct characterization (a), (c). Therefore, (d) is incorrect.

29. A: Chopin uses direct characterization in this paragraph by telling readers that the character had never considered marriage, never been in love; declined a proposal years ago, and had not yet lived to regret it. This directly tells readers about this aspect of her character. Indirect (b) characterization would instead show readers about it through the character's actions, thoughts, and/or words, and/or those of other characters. Since (a) is correct and (b) is incorrect, (c) and (d) are also incorrect.

30. C: This paragraph includes mainly description, but there is also a little bit of indirect characterization; thus, (a) is incorrect. The character does not say anything or do much in this paragraph to reveal her character; thus, (b) and (d) are both incorrect. Her having a dog, being religious, and shooting chicken-hawks herself with her gun are elements of indirect characterization. The rest of the paragraph is description establishing setting and situation more than character—i.e., she owned a farm and employed farmhands.

31. B: The first device Tennyson opens with is repetition, of the phrase "Half a league," three times. He uses a metaphor (a) second, in "the valley of Death," an implicit comparison of death to a valley. He does not use hyperbole (c), which is extreme exaggeration for effect, or imagery (d), i.e., descriptions that evoke mental images—visual, auditory, and/or of other senses—as his first device (though "the valley of Death" is a poetic image as well as a metaphor, this is used second, not first).

32. D: The sound of the first two lines creates a rhythm reminiscent of soldiers marching, which is their subject, by repeating dactylic (/ᴗᴗ) and trochaic (/ᴗ) beats. The phrase "half a league" refers to how far they must march (c. 1.5 miles); repeating this does not minimize the distance (b), but emphasizes it as well as establishing the mood of the soldiers' weariness (c).

33. C: The phrase "the valley of Death" not only reminds readers of the Old Testament's Psalm 23 ("The Lord is my shepherd")'s famous line, "Yea, though I walk through the valley of the shadow of death…," (a) it also uses a metaphor (b), i.e., an implicit comparison, of death to a valley, rather than a simile (d), i.e., an explicit comparison (e.g., "death is *like* a valley").

34. A: This stanza uses primarily dactylic (/ᴗᴗ) dimeter (two beats per line). The first two lines rhyme as a couplet (AA); the third and fourth do not (BC); the fifth, sixth, and seventh lines are a rhymed triplet (DDD); the eighth line does not rhyme with others (E); and the ninth line is a near rhyme (aka slant rhyme) with the fourth (C). Iambic pentameter (b) would be five beats per line of (ᴗ /). Trochaic tetrameter (c) would be four beats per line of (/ ᴗ). Anapestic heptameter (d) would be seven beats per line of (ᴗ ᴗ /) (an example is most lines of Poe's "Annabel Lee").

35. B: These lines do not involve a lot of variety (a). Rather, they contain very simple, short words—only two with two syllables, the rest all with one—as well as consistent rhythm. Also, all three lines begin with the same word ("Theirs"), and all three end with rhyming words ("reply, why, die"). This simplicity reflects the meaning that the soldiers do not talk back to their superiors, and do not conjecture about rationales for the battle, but simply do their jobs, which often include dying. These lines are not irregular (c) in rhyme, meter, word choice, word length, etc. Though regular, they are not monotonous (d); in fact, they are some of the most famous, oft-quoted lines from the poem.

36. B: Imagery is description accessing readers' senses so they feel they are experiencing what is described; e.g., in his long poem *The Waste Land,* T. S. Eliot conveys a civilization's decay through images of dried-up wells, crumbling towers, and toppled tombstones. A simile (a) is an explicit comparison using "like" or "as," etc., e.g. Wordsworth's "I wandered lonely as a cloud" in "Daffodils." A metaphor (c) is an implicit comparison, e.g., Longfellow's "O Ship of State." Hyperbole (d)

61

deliberately exaggerates for effect, e.g., Mark Twain's "I... could have hung my hat on my eyes, they stuck out so far."

37. D: Onomatopoeia refers to words that sound like what they represent. For example, the word *hum* (a) resembles the sound people or things make when they hum. *Click* (b) replicates the sound effect that it identifies. *Buzz* (c), like *hum*, contains phonemes similar to the sounds made by bees, buzzers, etc. However, *dog* (d), a noun naming a specific animal subspecies, is not onomatopoetic (although words for its vocalizations, e.g., "bow-wow," "arf," "woof," etc. are).

38. B: When students learn to summarize text, they learn to identify the most important ideas in a text AND organize those ideas in their minds (a); identify the themes, problems, and solutions in the text (b); monitor reading comprehension; AND correctly sequence (c) story events, essay points, etc. Graphic organizers, drawing, and other visuals help students visualize connections more than summarizing (d), a more mental and verbal than visual activity (though such visualization can aid summarization).

39. A: Criteria for evaluating the strength of a prediction based on textual evidence include that the very best analysis shows special insight into a theme, character trait, or change; and that the best evidence to support this insight is strong, relevant, and accurate. Analysis that suffices but is not best shows reasonable understanding supported by relevant, clear, and accurate, if not strong, evidence (b). Analysis only partially meeting criteria shows reasonable understanding, but its supporting evidence is generalized, only partially relevant or accurate (c), or weakly connected. Analysis showing only generalized or vague understanding, even with relevant and accurate supporting evidence (d), is insufficient.

40. A: Both groups of students most likely will find both texts conflict in their perspectives on the given topics. Lincoln opposed slavery, Douglas supported it; the two debated this topic while running for president. The Romantic movement was an opposite reaction against the Enlightenment: the latter promoted rationalism, the former emotionalism. Their views of nature differed: Enlightenment thinkers sought to study it objectively, believing they could impose order; Romantics sought to celebrate its chaotic, complex potential, believing they could never completely understand or control it. Hence, both pairs would conflict, not one (b). They would unlikely be similar (c). Neither would differ only slightly (d).

41. B: This is an example of a metaphor, i.e., an implicit comparison that equates two different things (the Great Depression and a cloud). Option (a) is an example of a simile, i.e., an explicit comparison that equates two different things by using *like* or *as*. Options (c) and (d) are both examples of using literal rather than figurative language, i.e., describing things without comparing them to anything else.

42. A, C, and E: An "onslaught" (a) literally means a vigorous attack or onset, as of criticism here. A "throng" (c) literally means a multitude of people or things assembled/crowded together, as of onlookers here. "Belligerent" literally means hostile, and "mob" (e) literally means an unruly crowd. However, "avalanche" (b) literally means a large snow or ice slide; figuratively it means any sudden, overwhelming amount or occurrence, as with rumors here. A "gaggle" (d) literally refers to a flock of geese; figuratively it can be used to describe a group pejoratively, as with women here.

43. A: Authors do not overtly or explicitly state everything in texts, including informational ones; hence readers need to draw inferences to fill in unstated information. Drawing inferences helps readers both to answer more questions about a text and understand it better (b). To make inferences, readers must not only know the information in the text, they must also add it to their prior knowledge (c). Drawing inferences about text can produce subjective or objective interpretations or both (d).

44. C: Some inferences that would be most suitable for a reader to draw about a nonfictional biography or autobiography include regarding the subject's actions and activities (a), events described in the text (b), and the message the author wants to communicate (d). However, inferences about problems and solutions described (c) are more suitable when reading a nonfiction informational or expository text.

45. C: To understand, critically judge, draw conclusions about, and make their own interpretations of informational text they read, students must be able to locate evidence in a text, organize the information (a), not only organize information but differentiate (b) whether it contains main ideas or details (c), make inferences about the text, and connect it to their prior knowledge (d).

46. D: Giving students sentence frames (a) (e.g., "A _____ is a(n) _____, so..." for students to complete, e.g., "A rabbit is a herbivore, so it eats only plants"; "A frog is a carnivore, so it eats only meat," etc.) will help students analyze author comparison and contrast of categories. Cloze procedures (b) are essentially the same: they present incomplete sentences for students to fill in the blanks. These are more effective than memorizing the terms (c) carnivore, herbivore, and omnivore and their definitions, as students learn meanings accompanied by reasoning processes rather than rote memorization.

47. C: One of the advantages of portfolio assessments is that they can be used as formative assessments (a), summative assessments (b), or both (c). For example, a teacher can review a student's latest writing sample in a portfolio to gauge current performance levels, compare it to the one immediately before it, monitor progress, etc. as formative assessment (a); review all contents of a portfolio collected over an entire school year to assess overall achievement as summative assessment (b); or both (c). Thus option (d) is incorrect.

48. A: Ad hominem is Latin for "against the man." Another way of describing this tactic is "shooting the messenger." This means the person doing the persuading impugns the message by association with the person delivering it. Examples of the persuasion technique used in the media that involves majority belief (b) are expressions such as "Five million people can't be wrong" or "Four out of five dentists recommend this brand." Scapegoating (c) is blaming one person/group for problems far too complex to attribute to any single individual/group. Using denial (d) is a way to accuse one's opponent without taking responsibility for it, e.g., "I won't mention my opponent's history of legal problems."

49. C: *The* is a definite article because it refers to a specific noun. *A* (a) and *an* (b) are indefinite articles, which refer to nonspecific nouns. For example, "Let's read *a* book" means let's read any book; "Let's read *the* book" means let's read a certain, specified book. Therefore, (d) is incorrect.

50. D: This is an example of nonparallel structure. The first three verbs ("hiking, swimming, rowing") are gerunds (verb participles ending with –*ing,* used as nouns—in this sentence, they are direct objects). Then suddenly the fourth verb ("to climb mountains") is an infinitive. It does not match the others, creating a lack of parallel structure. The sentence should read either "hiking, swimming, rowing, and climbing mountains" or "to hike, to swim, to row, and to climb mountains"/ "to hike, swim, row, and climb mountains."

51. C: First, the past tense of *to see* is *saw,* not *seen. Seen* is the perfect form, used in present perfect, past perfect, and future perfect tenses, e.g., "I have seen," "I had seen," and "I will have seen." Second, the possessive form of the pronoun *it* is *its,* not *it's. It's* is ONLY used as a contraction of *it is,* e.g., "It's raining." An apostrophe is used with possessive proper nouns, e.g., "This is Mary's book," and with possessive nouns, e.g., "This is the teacher's book." However, apostrophes are NOT used with possessive pronouns, e.g., "This is yours," "this is hers," "this is his," or "this is ours."

52. B: Boldface is a text feature most often used to indicate words that are also listed and defined in the glossary, emphasizing them so students notice them more easily and know they can look up their definitions. A footnote (a) is indicated by a superscript number[1] at the end of the word or sentence, not by **boldface.** Captions (c) below or beside visuals, explaining them, are not in **boldface.** Neither is the text in sidebars (d), i.e., boxes at one side of a page with added information, often in more focus or depth.

53. A: Rubrics are useful for identifying learning objectives, guiding student work, AND teacher assessment of student work. Teachers should explain a rubric to students before they begin work (b). Then the students should use the rubric components to guide their work (a). Once they have finished, the teachers should use the rubric to assess (c) whether students met all learning objectives included in the rubric. Teachers create or select rubrics to match learning objectives they have identified in their lesson plans, not to organize those lesson plans (d).

54. C: Two equally effective ways to teach students the difference between denotations and connotations are (a) to provide sample sentences, e.g., using the word "challenge" in a sentence and students must choose among (A) easy (B) hard (C) fun (D) needing effort as the meaning, based on sentence context; or (b) to teach the difference by using the same word in different sentence contexts to illustrate positive or negative connotations, e.g., "I rose to the challenge by competing" vs. "The contest was too big a challenge for me to win." Therefore, choice (d) is incorrect.

55. A, B, and E: Although science professors traditionally warned science students to avoid using the active voice and the first person (a) in technical writing, most modern editors of science journals and books dislike the weakness and dullness of the passive voice (b); many science journal articles alternate, so either or both are acceptable. Sentence (c) is an example of overly self-deprecating mood, sentence (d) is an example of overly grandiose mood, and sentence (e) is an example of an ideal balance between the two.

56. A: Description (b) explicitly states the students' emotional status and their reason for it, plus indicates via "just because" that they overreacted. Description (c) explicitly states only the objective part of the situation, neither explicitly nor implicitly addressing the students' subjective reaction. Description (d) explicitly states both the students' inward emotion and outward sign of it. Only description (a) implies their inward emotion by describing only the outward sign.

57. C: The student should consult a grammar guide to determine whether written sentences are complete and correct. An encyclopedia (a) gives comprehensive information on various content subjects and may include grammatical topics, but it will not explicitly define or explain all rules of syntax and grammar. A dictionary (b) gives the correct spellings, pronunciations, parts of speech, meanings, and origins of vocabulary words rather than grammatical rules. The grammar-check feature of a word-processor program (d) is a poor choice because its information is incomplete, it lacks human understanding, and its "corrections" are wrong more often than not; moreover, the student would have to type sentences into the word processor for feedback, but he or she could not use it to look up grammar rules.

58. A: When informational text authors do not explicitly state their point of view or purpose, readers should ask themselves and try to answer these four things: what the author wants to persuade readers to agree with or believe (b), how the author's word choices affect reader perceptions of the subject matter (a), how author choices of examples and/or facts affect reader perceptions of the subject matter (c), and what the author wanted to accomplish by writing the text (d).

59. B: Three nouns are included in the compound subject of this sentence, so the verb should be the plural "are," not the singular "is." There is only one verb, so any error of agreement between/among verb tenses (c) is impossible. Lack of parallel structure (d) involves disagreement among grammatical structures, e.g., "walking, running, and to jump" instead of "walking, running, and jumping." There is no such error in this sentence. Because (b) is correct, (a) is incorrect.

60. C: This is a compound sentence, i.e., one with two independent clauses that could each stand alone as a complete sentence, joined by a coordinating conjunction ("and"). A simple sentence (a) would have only one independent clause, not two. A complex sentence (b) would have an independent clause and a dependent clause. A compound–complex (d) sentence would include at least one dependent clause in addition to the two independent clauses.

61. D: A complex (a) sentence has at least one independent and one dependent clause. A compound (b) sentence has at least two independent clauses, but no dependent clauses. A compound–complex (c) sentence has at least two independent clauses, plus at least one dependent clause.

62. D: Version (a) has a compound structure, i.e., two independent clauses connected by coordinating conjunctions ("and so"). Version (b) has a complex structure, i.e., an independent clause plus a dependent clause ("because she was sick") that could not stand alone as a sentence but depends on the independent clause. Version (c) has a simple sentence structure; the single subject has a compound predicate with two verbs, but it is still only one independent clause. Version (d) is compound–complex, having two independent clauses ("She didn't attend" and "she missed the party") plus one dependent clause ("because she was sick").

63. A: This is a simple sentence, which is a single independent clause (containing a compound verb). Variation (b) is a complex sentence, which has a dependent clause ("Although you can run") that could not be a sentence on its own and depends on the independent clause ("you can't hide"), which could be a sentence by itself. Variation (c) is a compound sentence, which has two independent clauses joined by the coordinating conjunction "but." Variation (d) is a compound–complex sentence that includes two independent clauses ("Run" and "run fast"), each of which could be stand-alone sentences, and a dependent clause ("because you can't hide"), which could not.

64. C: This is a complex sentence. It has one independent clause ("He could not finish the test in time") and a dependent clause ("even though he tried his hardest"), which is subordinate to and depends on the independent clause. It is not a compound–complex (a) sentence, which would have two independent clauses and at least one dependent clause, because it has only one independent clause. It is not a compound (b) sentence, which has at least two independent clauses but no dependent clauses, because it has only one independent clause and does include a dependent clause. It is not a simple (d) sentence, which would be only one independent clause with no dependent clause.

65. B: Chomsky wrote this sentence to prove the point that correct syntax (a), mechanics (c), and grammar (d) are not enough to produce meaning; semantics (b) must also be correct. The sentence structure and word order are correct in his sentence (a); the period at the end is the only punctuation needed (c); and the verb "sleep" agrees with the plural subject "ideas" (d). However, the adjectives "Colorless" and "green" directly contradict each other: a noun cannot be both; and the adverb "furiously" is incompatible to modify the verb "sleep," which may be done peacefully, quietly, etc. or restlessly, fitfully, etc., but not furiously. Moreover, ideas do not sleep, except metaphorically (e.g., "The latent idea slept in his mind until an experience awakened it.") This sentence provides no context to establish/confirm such a metaphor.

66. B and C: There is no inconsistency of verb tense (a) in this sentence, nor is there any misplaced modifier (d). However, "To better serve you" is a split infinitive (b), which is easily corrected as "to serve you better," and the second comma creates a comma splice (c), i.e., incorrectly separating two independent clauses with a comma instead of the correct punctuation, a semicolon. Therefore, (e) is incorrect.

67. C: The first step the reader should take for evaluating argumentative writing is to identify what assumptions the author has made about the issue s/he discusses in the writing. Assumptions are things that the author accepts without proof. If an author's assumptions are incorrect or illogical, the ensuing argument will be flawed. Readers can be misled by argumentative writing if they do not identify the author's assumptions. The reader's second step is to identify what kinds of evidence the author has offered to support the argument (d). The reader should then take the third step of evaluating how relevant this evidence is (b). The fourth step for the reader is to evaluate how objective the author is about the issue discussed in the writing (a).

68. B: Reporting findings from case studies is a rhetorical means of providing evidence supporting author purposes, viewpoints, and/or claims in informational text. Relating personal anecdotes (a) is a rhetorical means of giving readers more authentic and accessible examples of points, and of appealing to reader emotions. Making analogies between ideas (c) is a rhetorical means of illuminating points and enabling readers to relate to them more easily. Using wording and description to convince readers what is right or wrong (d) is a rhetorical means of appealing to their moral and/or ethical values.

69. C: An oxymoron combines contrasting, usually contradictory terms to make sense in an unusual, complex way, often enabling deeper exploration of semantics, like "cold fire" or the examples in the question. Hyperbole (a) is unrealistically exaggerated overemphasis for effect. A hyperbaton (b) uses unconventional syntax to add intrigue and complexity. Chiasmus (d) is two parallel yet inverted phrases or clauses (e.g., JFK's "Ask not what your country can do for you; ask what you can do for your country.")

70. A: One method of appeal is using generalizations nobody can disagree with, e.g., "We all want peace, not war." Authors can then make these appear to support more specific related arguments, e.g., to invade or withdraw from another country. Rhetorical questions (b) need no answers but force agreement, e.g., "Wouldn't you rather be paid more than less?" Transfer and association (c) persuade readers through example, e.g., advertising products enjoyed by attractive actors whom audiences would emulate. Humor can relax readers into agreement, but when it ridicules opponents (d) it can backfire, alienating readers not already agreeing.

71. B: Students should write appropriately to the specific occasion, purpose, and audience to ensure their particular readers will understand what they want to communicate. Therefore, writers in middle school grades should not use more advanced handwriting to set an example for younger readers (a); use longer, more complex sentences to give younger readers a challenge (c); or simply use their own typical levels to make their writing its most natural (d). They should instead use printing, simpler vocabulary and sentence structure, and shorter sentences on the level of readers in the early elementary grades. The primary goal is for the younger readers to understand the writing, so it should be at their reading levels.

72. C: It is most appropriate for students to write using more casual language on their own age level when writing for classmates. This applies whether they are writing narrative, argumentation, exposition, or speculation. When students want to share a particular experience with their readers (a), they should write using descriptive form, rather than persuasive or explanatory form, for example. Age/reading level will be determined by the audience. When students want permission for a desired activity (b), they should write using persuasive form, with mature, serious diction and more sophisticated vocabulary to appeal to parents. To write a story that younger children can read (d), they should write in narrative form, using simpler vocabulary and sentence structure; shorter sentences; more vivid, entertaining word choices; a lighter tone; and humor when appropriate.

73. D: One way writers fail to develop paragraphs sufficiently is omitting necessary background information. Omitting definitions of important terms and/or contexts for others' ideas is another cause of paragraphs that are underdeveloped, rather than lacking focus (c). Descriptions of settings, supporting evidence, and specific details are also necessary for adequate paragraph development. Paragraphs with generalizations but no details are hence undeveloped or underdeveloped, rather than unfocused (b). When the sentences within one paragraph seem unrelated, the paragraph is poorly focused rather than poorly developed (a). Lack of transitions between ideas, and including too many ideas in one paragraph, are additional sources of unfocused/inadequately focused paragraphs.

74. B: The paragraph structural pattern of narration (a) tells readers a story or part of one. The structural pattern of description (b) shows readers instead of telling them. The classification (c) pattern groups individual objects, beings, or ideas into categories by similarity, commonality, or according to an inclusive principle. The pattern of giving examples (d) illustrates points or ideas instead of telling, showing, or grouping them.

75. B: Readers *should* paraphrase an informational text, or summarize it or make an outline of it using their own words, to facilitate critically evaluating its effectiveness; research any subjects or vocabulary unfamiliar to them (b); consider which types of appeals the author uses as well as their effects (c); and evaluate how well the author communicates meaning from the *reader's* perspective, not what they presume is the author's perspective (d).

76. A: Although authors may state their purposes for writing informational text, some authors may leave unstated some equally important purposes (b). The main or central idea of a text is what the reader should understand from it, whereas the purpose of that text is why the author wrote it and/or what s/he wants readers to do with its information (c). By identifying unstated author purposes for texts, readers can evaluate text effectiveness better and judge whether they agree or disagree with it and why, which are all advantages (d).

77. A: A verb most often forms the predicate, which indicates an activity or state, including related words. For example, in "She went to the store," "went" is the verb and "to the store" is a prepositional phrase modifying the verb. A noun (b) most often forms the subject, i.e., the agent or experiencer of the predicate (in the preceding example, "She" is the subject). An adjective (c) most often modifies and describes a noun or another adjective. An adverb (d) most often modifies and describes a verb, an adjective, or another adverb.

78. B: Both "quickly" (a) and "carefully" (c) are adverbs in this sentence that modify the verb "completed," describing how she completed the task. "Challenging" (d) is an adjective; it modifies the noun "task," describing what the task was like or one of its characteristics.

79. D: When citing electronic sources, researchers must include the date they accessed the source in their references. When citing both printed and electronic sources, researchers must include the name of the author (a), the date of publication (b), and the title of the book or article (c).

80. B: The *MLA Style Manual* of the Modern Language Association is most commonly used for research papers on English literature. The *Publication Manual of the American Psychological Association* (APA) (a) is most commonly used for research papers in psychology, sociology, and the other social sciences. *The Chicago Manual of Style* (c) is almost identical to Kate Turabian's style manual (d), entitled *A Manual for Writers of Research Papers, Theses, and Dissertations,* both published by the University of Chicago Press. The only differences are minor modifications addressing the particular needs of students writing papers for courses. Although some instructors prefer and assign Turabian or Chicago style, MLA style is most often preferred for English literature papers.

81. B: Quoting other writers is a good technique for incorporating outside sources into a research paper, but students are advised to keep quotations brief. Longer quotations (c)—e.g., 6–8 long excerpts within a 10-page paper—are excessive. Students sometimes do this to pad their paper length, but they end up with more of others' material than their own. Students should also avoid ending their papers with quotations (a). This can be a ploy to prevent readers from challenging their assertions, to avoid thinking critically and considering multiple alternatives regarding the topic, and/or to avoid writing anything more in their own words about it. Quotations are better used to generate discussion than to suppress it. Students should also quote sources that both support and refute their assertions, not only the former (d). Readers with normal skepticism can more readily agree with writers' positions when they present evidence on both sides of an issue.

82. D: Nonverbal behaviors during speeches influence the listeners' perceptions of the speaker's competence, good character, trustworthiness, and therefore credibility. Speakers should make eye contact with everybody in the audience, not just certain listeners (a). Their body movements should not be random or unrelated (b) to what they are saying (e.g., pacing, face rubbing, playing with one's hair, tapping pencils or toes, etc.), but they should reinforce their verbal messages. Facial expressions should not be startling or unexpected (c); they should be consistent with both the verbal content and the speaker's vocal tones. A speaker's gestures should also be congruent with the meaning (d) of what s/he is saying, to fit with and emphasize the points they are communicating.

83. D: Mobile and text media are very popular (a) and increasingly so, an advantage for effective public communications. Another advantage of text messaging using mobile phones is the timeliness (b) with which information and reminders can be sent. Especially for public communications intended to effect social change, their interactive (c) potential is an additional advantage. Other advantages include decreasing costs and increasing rural reach. One disadvantage of this media format is the limited length (d) to which messages are restricted. However, most presenters work around this disadvantage by inserting hyperlinks to websites/webpages for accessing further information. Other disadvantages include provider charges, although today, more providers are including free texting in mobile plans.

84. B: Although today digital text, images, and sound files can be reliably saved for longer periods of time, digital media are still not necessarily as permanent (a) or long lasting in the same form as text printed on paper, art painted on canvas, or music recorded in some other formats. However, digital media are more versatile (c): they can be displayed globally in multiple locations, on smartphones, palm devices, laptop screens, desktop monitors, giant public video screens, etc. They are more flexible (d): they can be sharpened, blurred, darkened, lightened; parts can be deleted, restored, duplicated, recombined, transposed, etc.; and changed/adapted for students with diverse needs. They can combine text, video, and audio, which print media cannot; enable students with learning challenges to select the most adaptive formats; and allow multimedia interactivity.

85. D: This description involves both an expert opinion (a) because the woman is identified as a doctor who recommends the prescription and a testimonial (b) because this doctor also identifies herself as a satisfied user of the product. It does not involve a bandwagon (c) appeal, which cites use of a brand by a majority of consumers to persuade others to join them.

86. C: The bandwagon method appeals to audiences to use a brand because it is popular, implying popularity indicates quality. Past Dr Pepper® commercials sang, "I'm a pepper, he's a pepper, she's a pepper…. Wouldn't you like to be a pepper, too?" Associating a car with a beautiful model (a), a soap with a waterfall (b), or a USA-made brand with an American flag (d) are all examples of the transfer method of appeal: viewers transfer the feelings they get from symbols to associated products and (unconsciously/consciously) want the products to get those feelings.

87. C: Statistics cited and examples given most represent evidence that writers supply to support the claims they make in written arguments. Claims (a) are the writer's basic positions regarding the topic. Reasons (b) also support claims as evidence does; however, evidence involves statistics, specific examples, or other facts from different sources that demonstrate the claim's validity, whereas reasons are given by the writer (e.g., for a claim that overusing digital devices causes harm, a reason could be that texting while driving causes accidents). Counterclaims (d) are claims that refute/oppose/contradict given claims.

88. A = 2: Argumentum ad populum, appeal/argument to the public, is fallacious by citing public agreement with something, which does not necessarily prove it is right. B = 3: Argumentum ad ignorantiam, appeal/argument to ignorance by assuming something true simply because it has never been proven false, is fallacious. C = 4: Argumentum ad nauseam, simply repeating something over and over to the point of nauseating one's audience without any added proof or support, is fallacious. D = 1: Argumentum ad verecundiam, appeal/argument to authority, is fallacious when someone uses an authority in one field to prove something in an unrelated field in which that authority has no expertise.

89. C: Citing evidence of only one budget cut (a), even though it is the largest, is not sufficient evidence because it does not represent a significant proportion of all community colleges in the state. Similarly, citing only two examples (b), regardless of their prominence, does not represent a significant proportion of the total. Citing examples from 15 of 34 colleges (c) in the state shows that the general claim is true for a significant proportion of community colleges in the state. Citing specific cut amounts at all 34 colleges (d) is beyond sufficient, to the point of excess: reading/listening audiences would likely be so bored by this amount of evidence, it would distract them from accepting the claim.

90. D: This non-sentence has no predicate, making it a fragment. Thus choice (a) is incorrect. "Going" is a gerund (a verb participle used as a noun) and the sentence subject, not the verb. Replacing the comma with the copula or linking verb "is" (or "was," "will," "can," "could," "would be," etc.) would correct it. An example of lack of parallelism (c) would be "Going to the beach is more enjoyable than to stay home." Correction: either "To go to the beach" and "to stay home" OR "Going to the beach" and "staying home."

91. B: Research findings show that it helps ELL students for teachers to assign them in pairs, particularly for projects (a), experiments, and reports; to write problems and directions for them using shorter, simpler sentences (b); to emphasize student work accuracy much more than student work speed (c); and to ask ELL students many questions that they must use higher level cognitive processes to answer (d).

92. D: The CALLA is a content-based approach to language instruction that integrates academic learning strategies that students require to participate in mainstream English-speaking classrooms. It includes objectives for content (a), language (b), and learning strategies (c), and it allows teachers to plan lessons using content based on themes or formats using sheltered content (d).

93. C: Teachers must establish and communicate clear ground rules for students before initiating collaborative classroom discussions. One rule is to prohibit cross talk, which is counterproductive to equitable conversations. Another rule for teachers to set is that students should not interrupt other students when they are speaking (a). An additional good rule is to caution talkative students not to monopolize the conversation (b). Teachers should not only set a ground rule against verbal abuse of classmates, they should additionally set a rule against physical abuse (e.g., shoving, hitting, kicking, biting, etc.), which is not unlikely (d) with younger students and students with behavioral issues.

94. D: With possessive adjectives, do NOT use an apostrophe: "Your" and "its" are correct. Choice (a) incorrectly adds an apostrophe to both possessive adjectives; choice (b) uses "Your" correctly, but "it's" is incorrect; choice (c) uses "You're" incorrectly but "its" correctly. "You're" and "it's" can ONLY be contractions of "you are" and "it is," respectively.

95. C: Longer sentences are not necessarily clauses, and shorter sentences are not necessarily phrases. A clause can stand alone as a sentence, has a subject and verb, and no subordinating conjunction, relative pronoun, or other subordinating word or phrase making it dependent. Choices (a) and (b) each have a subject and a verb, and are clauses; choice (d) has an adverb, subject, verb, and preposition, and is a clause. However, choice (c) is a noun phrase containing an article, adverb, adjective, and noun, but no verb.

96. A: Students can post, read, and comment on blog posts at home and in school, facilitating homework and classroom discussion. Podcasts (b) can stimulate dialogues between their creators and viewers, but as download files, they preclude dynamic interactions such as class discussions. RSS feeds (c) are good for students/teachers to read teachers'/other students' posts, but they are typically unilateral, not permitting interactive discussion online. Videoconference (d) does enable online communication, but only in real time, and content is not easy to retrieve or saved automatically.

97. A: The meaning of *trans-* as "across" can be discerned based on vocabulary words like *transport* (carry across), *translate* and *transfer* (both meaning to bear or carry across), *transgender* (across gender), *transition* (crossing or going across), *transduce* (to convert across forms, e.g., of energy), etc. All these share the common prefix meaning of across or from one place or thing to another. One prefix meaning "change" (b) is *meta-* (e.g., metamorphosis). *Port-* as in "portable" means carry (c). A prefix meaning "different" (d) is *hetero-* (e.g., heterosexual, heterogeneous, heterocyclic, heteromorphic).

98. C: Prewriting strategies (a) include helping students generate ideas, organize them, access their background knowledge, identify research topics, and use graphics to visualize ideas. Modeling strategies (b) include teacher demonstration, giving students exemplary models of expected writing types, helping students analyze models, and inviting students to emulate effective model elements in their writing. Process writing (d) includes giving students opportunities for extended practice, peer interaction, personal responsibility, writing for authentic audiences, and self-evaluation. Inquiry strategies (c) include setting clear goals, observing concrete data, and applying learning.

99. A: A primary characteristic of informative or explanatory writing is that the author assumes certain things to be factual or true. From these assumptions, the author proceeds to inform readers, explain things to them, and offer them insights. Descriptive (b) writing uses multiple sensory details to paint a picture for readers so they can feel they are experiencing what is described. Persuasive (c) writing endeavors to convince readers something is true rather than assuming it is. Narrative (d) writing relates a story or stories to readers.

100. A, B, and D: The What Works Clearinghouse (WWC) reports strong research evidence for giving students explicit vocabulary instruction (a) and explicit and direct instruction in reading comprehension strategies (b) and for giving struggling readers intensive, individualized interventions by trained specialists (d). The WWC reports research findings of moderate evidence for getting students more motivated for and engaged in learning reading (c) and for giving students opportunities to engage in extended discussions of text meanings and interpretations (e).

101. D: Research-based recommendations from the COI include teaching students how to use effective reading comprehension strategies—as well as giving them supportive practice in using them—throughout the school day (a); setting and sustaining high standards for text, vocabulary, AND questions and conversation (b); focusing equally on raising student motivation to read and student engagement with reading (c); and instructing students in the content knowledge they need to master concepts crucial to their comprehension and learning (d).

102. D: Common purposes for writing in journals include working through feelings, e.g., grief, for therapeutic reasons; documenting experiences with the writer's or another's terminal illness (a); chronicling experiences with recovery from addiction (b); and describing travels to and/or life in other countries or spiritual journals (c). However, relating stories of fictional plots and characters (d) is commonly achieved through writing novels, novellas, and short stories rather than journals.

103. C: For teaching middle school students effective writing strategies, teachers need to give explicit instruction in specific tasks such as steps in writing argumentative essays (a) and in more general processes such as brainstorming, editing, etc. (b); teachers also should give explicit instruction in planning before writing and in revising and editing during writing (d). Explicit instruction is equally important to teach effective strategies for all of these.

104. B: When teachers assign cooperative writing partnerships, each student in a pair should not always take only one role (a); they must both take turns writing and reviewing their partner's writing (b) to experience both roles in the process. Each student should provide not only positive feedback (c) or only constructive feedback (d) to a partner, but both. For example, if the assignment is using descriptive adjectives, positive feedback would be identifying specific descriptive adjectives the partner used; constructive feedback could be identifying sentences that could use more descriptive adjectives.

105. D: According to experts, punctuation is even *more* important online than in print (a). Beginners are advised to start with shorter sentences. Blog paragraphs should be *much shorter* than print paragraphs (b), like two to six sentences each, because reading online is more difficult. Writers should leave enough blank space (c) because readers' eyes and brains tire from overly busy web pages. Because online readers often approach blog posts in varying orders, bloggers should write consistently throughout each post, telling a story with a beginning, middle, and end (d).

106. C: Summative assessments are administered after instruction and less often than formative assessments, which teachers make more frequently during instruction (a) to inform changes to make their teaching more effective (b). Typical times for summative assessments are after each lesson, unit, and school year is completed (c). Teachers rely on formative, not summative assessments for individual student data (d); they rely on summative assessment results for group data and group comparisons.

107. A: Formative assessments are most often criterion-referenced tests, which measure a student's performance against a predetermined criterion that indicates success or proficiency. They are typically not norm-referenced tests (b), which measure a student's performance against the average performance (scores) of normative sample student groups, such as standardized tests used as summative assessments. Formative assessments may occasionally be standardized, but most frequently they are informal measures (c). They are not the most objective (d)—formal tests are—but formative assessments are better for monitoring student progress, evaluating teacher effectiveness, and informing instructional adjustments.

108. B: Questionnaires (a) typically use short-answer items such as yes/no questions/statements, Likert scales measuring within a range of agreement/disagreement, like/dislike, etc. rather than open-ended requests for reflective comments or feedback. Having students rate teachers (c) is inappropriate because the focus is on curriculum and assessment design and use, not on a teacher's performance. Assigning essays (d) is more likely to obtain students writing about the subject matter itself rather than their reflective responses. Having students write in journals (b) enables them to reflect on their course matter and tests and record these reflections, which teachers can then read.

109. D: Although there are many ready-made rubrics available online free of charge, and a teacher's selecting one this way eliminates added work (a), it does nothing to incorporate student input. Although the teacher knows the learning objectives and how to create a rubric, the teacher is not the only one who should do it (b): collaborating with students will not only ensure that they know and understand the learning objectives as well as teach them how to design rubrics, but it will also incorporate their input and feedback about curriculum and assessment into the design. Rather than collecting student input and then creating the rubric alone (c), the teacher should work together with all students to incorporate their input (d).

110. A: Students who want to get readers to agree with them should use argumentation or persuasion. Those wanting to relate a story and the lesson to learn from it should use narrative writing (b). Those wanting to invite readers to explore ideas with them should use speculative writing (c). Students wanting to share an experience with readers should use descriptive writing (d) to make it more real.

72

Thank You

We at Mometrix would like to extend our heartfelt thanks to you, our friend and patron, for allowing us to play a part in your journey. It is a privilege to serve people from all walks of life who are unified in their commitment to building the best future they can for themselves.

The preparation you devote to these important testing milestones may be the most valuable educational opportunity you have for making a real difference in your life. We encourage you to put your heart into it—that feeling of succeeding, overcoming, and yes, conquering will be well worth the hours you've invested.

We want to hear your story, your struggles and your successes, and if you see any opportunities for us to improve our materials so we can help others even more effectively in the future, please share that with us as well. **The team at Mometrix would be absolutely thrilled to hear from you!** So please, send us an email (support@mometrix.com) and let's stay in touch.

If you feel as though you need additional help, please check out the other resources we offer:

> **Study Guide: http://MometrixStudyGuides.com/GACE**
>
> **Flashcards: http://MometrixFlashcards.com/GACE**

74